THE OFFICIAL
U.S. ARMY
CIVIL
DISTURBANCES
HANDBOOK

UPDATED

RIOT & CROWD CONTROL STRATEGY & TACTICS

CURRENT, FULL-SIZE EDITION

ATP 3-39.33
(FM 3-19.15)

April 2014
Headquarters, Department of the Army

The Official US Army Civil Disturbances Handbook - Updated

Riot & Crowd Control Strategy & Tactics - Current, Full-Size Edition - Giant 8.5" x 11" Format: Large, Clear Print & Pictures - ATP 3-39.33 (FM 3-19.15)

U.S. Army

This edition first published 2018 by Carlile Military Library. "Carlile Military Library" and its associated logos and devices are trademarks. Carlile Military Library is an imprint of Carlile Media. The appearance of U.S. Department of Defense (DoD) visual information does not imply or constitute DoD endorsement.

New material copyright © 2018 Carlile Media. **All rights reserved.**

Published in the United States of America.

ISBN-13: 978-1-9875-7546-0
ISBN-10: 1987575466

Army Techniques Publication
No. 3-39.33

*ATP 3-39.33

Headquarters
Department of the Army
Washington, DC, 21 April 2014

Civil Disturbances

Contents

		Page
	PREFACE	v
	INTRODUCTION	vi
Chapter 1	**OPERATIONAL THREATS**	**1-1**
	Civil Unrest	1-1
	Crowd Development	1-2
	Crowd Dynamics	1-3
	Behavior Theories	1-4
	Crowd Types	1-6
	Crowd Tactics	1-7
Chapter 2	**CONTROL FORCE PLANNING AND TACTICS**	**2-1**
	Planning Considerations	2-1
	Graduated Response	2-8
	Planning a Graduated-Response Matrix	2-10
	Nonlethal Weapons	2-12
	Crowd Management Tactics	2-14
	Apprehension Teams	2-20
Chapter 3	**EQUIPMENT AND TECHNIQUES**	**3-1**
	Riot Shield and Riot Baton	3-1
	Additional Protective Equipment	3-16
	Team Work	3-18
Chapter 4	**CONTROL FORCE FORMATIONS**	**4-1**
	General Information	4-1
	Actions Before Movement	4-2
	Actions at Rally Point	4-2
	Formations	4-3
	Extraction Teams	4-7
	Lethal Overwatch Teams	4-8
	Reserve Forces	4-8
	Squad Formations	4-9
	Platoon Formations With Three Squads	4-11
	Platoon Formations With Four Squads	4-19

Distribution Restriction: Approved for public release; distribution is unlimited.

*This publication supersedes FM 3-19.15, 18 April 2005.

Contents

	Company Formations	4-28
	Formations With Vehicles	4-33
	Additional Formations	4-37
Chapter 5	CONFINEMENT FACILITIES	5-1
	Crowd Dynamics	5-1
	Planning	5-2
	Control Force Formations	5-6
Appendix A	METRIC CONVERSION CHART	A-1
Appendix B	PRACTICAL APPLICATION	B-1
	GLOSSARY	Glossary-1
	REFERENCES	References-1
	INDEX	Index-1

Figures

Figure 2-1. Sample GRM card	2-9
Figure 2-2. Sample proclamation	2-18
Figure 2-3. Delaying tactic	2-20
Figure 3-1. Riot shield positions	3-2
Figure 3-2. Riot shield retention (top grab attempt)	3-2
Figure 3-3. Riot shield retention (bottom grab attempt)	3-3
Figure 3-4. Escalation of trauma chart	3-4
Figure 3-5. Riot batons	3-5
Figure 3-6. Vertical, high-profile carry	3-6
Figure 3-7. Vertical low profile	3-7
Figure 3-8. High block (steps 1 and 2)	3-8
Figure 3-9. Low block (steps 1 and 2)	3-8
Figure 3-10. Strong-side block (steps 1 and 2)	3-9
Figure 3-11. Middle block	3-10
Figure 3-12. Forward strike	3-11
Figure 3-13. Reverse strike	3-12
Figure 3-14. Two-hand, strong-side, horizontal strike	3-13
Figure 3-15. Two-hand, support-side, horizontal strike	3-13
Figure 3-16. Front jab	3-14
Figure 3-17. Rear jab	3-14
Figure 3-18. Two-hand, middle strike	3-15
Figure 3-19. Tracing-C technique	3-16
Figure 3-20. Nonballistic riot face shield	3-16
Figure 3-21. Shin guards	3-17
Figure 3-22. Ballistic riot shield	3-17
Figure 3-23. Weapon positions	3-19

Figure 4-1. Symbol key 4-1
Figure 4-2. Column formation 4-3
Figure 4-3. Hand-and-arm signals 4-5
Figure 4-4. Extraction team formation 4-7
Figure 4-5. Squad line formation 4-9
Figure 4-6. Squad echelon formations 4-9
Figure 4-7. Squad wedge formation 4-10
Figure 4-8. Squad diamond or circle formation 4-10
Figure 4-9. Platoon line formation (three squads) 4-11
Figure 4-10. Platoon line formation with general support 4-12
Figure 4-11. Platoon line formation with lateral support (right) 4-12
Figure 4-12. Platoon line formation with direct support 4-13
Figure 4-13. Platoon echelon left formation 4-14
Figure 4-14. Platoon echelon left formation with the 2d squad in general support 4-14
Figure 4-15. Platoon echelon left formation with the 2d squad in lateral support 4-15
Figure 4-16. Platoon echelon left formation with the 2d squad in direct support 4-15
Figure 4-17. Platoon wedge formation 4-16
Figure 4-18. Platoon wedge formation with 2d squad in general support 4-16
Figure 4-19. Platoon wedge formation with the 2d squad in lateral support 4-17
Figure 4-20. Platoon wedge formation with the 2d squad in lateral support (right) 4-17
Figure 4-21. Platoon wedge formation with the 2d squad in direct support 4-18
Figure 4-22. Platoon diamond formation 4-18
Figure 4-23. Platoon circle formation 4-19
Figure 4-24. Platoon line formation with four squads 4-20
Figure 4-25. Platoon line formation with 2d and 3d squads in general support 4-21
Figure 4-26. Platoon line formation with 2d and 3d squads in lateral support 4-22
Figure 4-27. Platoon line formation with 2d and 3d squads in direct support 4-22
Figure 4-28. Platoon echelon left formation with four squads 4-23
Figure 4-29. Platoon echelon left formation with 2d and 3d squads in general support 4-24
Figure 4-30. Platoon echelon left formation with 2d and 3d squads in lateral support . 4-24
Figure 4-31. Platoon echelon left formation with 2d and 3d squads in direct support .. 4-25
Figure 4-32. Platoon wedge formation with four squads 4-25
Figure 4-33. Platoon wedge formation with 2d and 3d squads in general support 4-26
Figure 4-34. Platoon wedge formation with 2d and 3d squads in lateral support 4-26
Figure 4-35. Platoon wedge formation with 2d and 3d squads in direct support 4-27
Figure 4-36. Company line in depth formation 4-28
Figure 4-37. Company line-in-mass formation 4-29
Figure 4-38. Company line mass formation with one platoon in depth 4-29
Figure 4-39. Company line-in-mass formation with one platoon in lateral support 4-29
Figure 4-40. Company line formation with one platoon in lateral support and one platoon in general support 4-30

Contents

Figure 4-41. Company echelon right formation with one platoon in lateral support and one platoon in general support 4-30
Figure 4-42. Company echelon right in mass formation with one platoon in lateral support 4-31
Figure 4-43. Company echelon left formation with one platoon in general support 4-31
Figure 4-44. Company echelon right in mass formation with one platoon in general support 4-32
Figure 4-45. Company wedge formation with two platoons in general support 4-32
Figure 4-46. Company wedge formation with one platoon in lateral support 4-33
Figure 4-47. Company wedge formation with one platoon in lateral support and one platoon in general support 4-33
Figure 4-48. Company column formation with vehicles 4-34
Figure 4-49. Company line formation with vehicles and two platoons in general support 4-34
Figure 4-50. Company line formation with vehicles, one platoon in lateral support and one platoon in general support 4-35
Figure 4-51. Company echelon left formation with vehicles, one platoon in lateral support and one platoon in general support 4-35
Figure 4-52. Company line-in-mass formation with vehicles and one platoon in general support 4-35
Figure 4-53. Platoon line formation with vehicles 4-36
Figure 4-54. Junction check (right) with platoon line formation 4-37
Figure 4-55. Open formation from a platoon line formation 4-38
Figure 5-1. Recording FCMT member duty position 5-9
Figure 5-2. Recording FCMT member equipment 5-9
Figure 5-3. Recording FCMT member number on armor 5-9
Figure 5-4. OIC with FCMT prior to cell entry 5-12
Figure B-1. Crowd massing B-2
Figure B-2. Early contact and unobtrusive crowd control measures B-3
Figure B-3. More obtrusive engagement as the crowd demonstrates negative indicators B-4
Figure B-4. Full engagement as crowd unlawfully demonstrates B-4

Tables

Table 2-1. Escalating situation crowd management techniques 2-14
Table 4-1. Control force basic commands 4-6
Table A-1. Metric conversion chart A-1

Preface

ATP 3-39.33 provides discussion and techniques about civil disturbances and crowd control operations that occur in the continental United States (CONUS) and outside the continental United States (OCONUS). United States (U.S.) forces deploy in support of unified action, overseas contingency operations, and humanitarian assistance worldwide. During these operations, U.S. forces are often faced with unruly and violent crowds who have the intent of disrupting peace and the ability of U.S. forces to maintain peace. Worldwide instability coupled with U.S. military participation in unified-action, peacekeeping, and related operations require that U.S. forces have access to the most current doctrine and techniques that are necessary to quell riots and restore public order.

The principal audience for ATP 3-39.33 is Army commanders and staff elements at all echelons who are tasked with planning and directing civil disturbance missions.

Commanders, staffs, and subordinates ensure that their decisions and actions comply with applicable U.S., international, and host nation (HN) laws and regulations. Commanders must ensure that Soldiers operate according to the law of war and the rules of engagement (ROE) (see FM 27-10).

Unless stated otherwise, masculine nouns or pronouns do not refer exclusively to men.

Appendix A contains a metric conversion chart for the measurements used in this manual. For a complete listing of preferred metric units for general use, see Fed-Std-376B.

ATP 3-39.33 uses joint terms where applicable. Selected joint and Army terms and definitions appear in both the glossary and the text. Terms for which ATP 3-39.33 is the proponent publication (the authority) are italicized in the text and are marked with an asterisk (*) in the glossary. Terms and definitions for which ATP 3-39.33 is the proponent publication are boldfaced in the text. For other definitions shown in the text, the term is italicized and the number of the proponent publication follows the definition.

ATP 3-39.33 applies to Active Army, Army National Guard/Army National Guard of the United States, and U.S. Army Reserve unless otherwise stated.

The proponent of ATP 3-39.33 is the U.S. Army Military Police School (USAMPS). The preparing agency is the Maneuver Support Center of Excellence (MSCoE) Capabilities Development and Integration Directorate; Concepts, Organizations, and Doctrine Development Division; Doctrine Branch. Send comments and recommendations on DA Form 2028 *(Recommended Changes to Publications and Blank Forms)* to Commander, MSCoE, ATTN: ATZT-CDC, 14000 MSCoE Loop, Suite 270, Fort Leonard Wood, MO 65473-8929; e-mail the DA Form 2028 to <usarmy.leonardwood.mscoe.mbx.cdidcodddmpdoc@mail.mil>; or submit an electronic DA Form 2028.

Introduction

Successful outcomes that follow civil disturbance situations are based on proper planning, Soldier and equipment employment, and on-the-ground decisions that are made by leaders and members of the control force who are face-to-face with an unruly, or potentially unruly, crowd. ATP 3-39.33 discusses and describes the techniques that are used by Army forces who are conducting civil deterrence or response missions to civil disturbances.

In the past century, there have been countless examples of civil disturbance situations around the world. The size and scope of these civil disturbances varied from small gatherings of people who were verbally protesting to full-blown riots that resulted in property destruction and violence against others. Over the past decade, law enforcement and professional experts have come to understand crowd dynamics. A better understanding of human behavior and crowd dynamics and technological advancement has led to improved responses to crowd control.

This publication covers a wide array of information that concerns civil disturbances along with the techniques that are used to quell or disperse those who are causing the disturbance. This publication discusses crowd dynamics and human behaviors, crowd types, control force basic equipment requirements, and control force formations. This publication also discusses planning requirements and recommendations and the legalities that are involved with civil disturbances and control forces.

This publication builds on the collective knowledge and wisdom that was gained through recent operations, numerous lessons learned, studies, and the deliberate process of informed reasoning throughout the Army. It is rooted in time-tested principles and fundamentals, while accommodating new technologies, human behavior, and organizational changes.

There are several changes from the 2005 version of this publication. These changes include the removal of chapter 3, chapter 5, and chapter 8 from the 2005 version. Due to doctrine content parameters and Doctrine 2015 guidelines, information on specific pieces of equipment and training has been removed.

The following is a brief introduction and summary of the chapters and appendixes in this publication:

- **Chapter 1.** Chapter 1 discusses the operational threats in a civil disturbance environment that leaders must understand to effectively combat them. This chapter also includes discussion on civil unrest, crowd dynamics and behavior, and tactics that are used within the various crowd types.
- **Chapter 2.** Chapter 2 addresses planning considerations and tactics that should be used by military units to employ the control force. Areas discussed include graduated response, nonlethal weapons (NLW), and legal considerations.
- **Chapter 3.** Chapter 3 provides recommendations for equipment types and techniques. This chapter focuses on the two primary pieces of equipment for a control force—the riot baton and riot shield. Additional protective equipment is also discussed, including how members of the control force work as a team while using the equipment.
- **Chapter 4.** Chapter 4 focuses on the control force and the different formations that can be utilized for crowd management. This chapter discusses the actions of the control force at different mission phases.
- **Chapter 5.** Chapter 5 addresses civil disturbances within confinement facilities and discusses crowd dynamics in the facility, planning considerations, and control force formations. This chapter also identifies specialized teams within a confinement facility and their purpose.
- **Appendix A.** Appendix A is a metric conversion chart.
- **Appendix B.** Appendix B applies the information given in this publication to a generic situation.

The foundations of civil disturbance operations that are provided in this manual support the actions and decisions of combatant commanders, staffs, and leaders at all levels. This publication is not meant to be a substitute for thought and initiative among leaders and Soldiers. No matter how robust the doctrine or how advanced the capabilities and systems, it is the Soldier who must understand the operational environment, recognize shortfalls, and adapt to the situation on the ground.

This publication is a military police doctrinal publication; however, it is geared toward any unit that may be tasked to respond to civil disturbances. Therefore, the diagrams used in this ATP (specifically those in chapter 4 that depict control force formations) are generic in nature. The formations can easily be modified to suit multiple-size squads, platoons, and companies. It is ultimately the decision of the commander on the ground as to how they will incorporate their units and Soldiers into formations.

This page intentionally left blank.

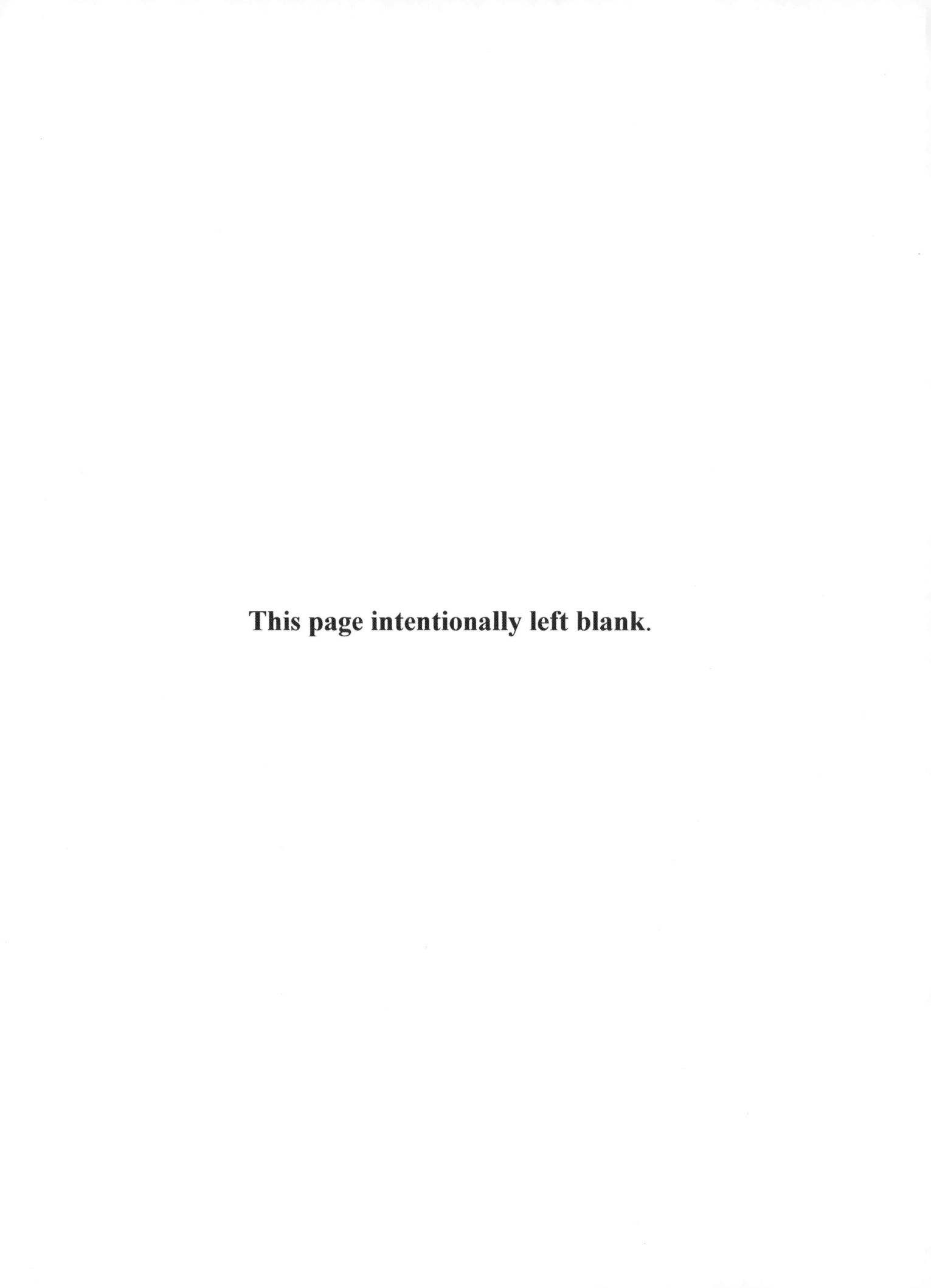

Chapter 1

Operational Threats

U.S. forces and unified-action partners face many threats from around the globe, including civil disturbances. The potential for instability exists in many regions across the world. After years of studying social strife, numerous factors can be pinpointed as potential sources for civil disturbances. Some of these factors are fluctuation of the world economy; competition for natural resources or basic human needs; and differing opinions on religion, politics, and human rights. History has shown that people everywhere demand to be treated fairly and want their grievances to be heard to right their perceived or real wrong. Often, U.S. forces have to respond to this type of situation and must know how their actions or inactions can affect the potential for threats.

CIVIL UNREST

1-1. Demonstrations, public disorder, and riots happen for a number of reasons. Some of these reasons are economic hardships, social injustices, ethnic differences (leading to oppression), objections to world organizations or certain governments, political grievances, terrorist acts, other man-made disasters, and natural disasters. Civil unrest is when a civil society or a segment of its population is in a disturbed or uneasy state or in turmoil. During a state of civil unrest, an event can be triggered by a single cause or a combination of causes. For example, operations that occurred in the Balkans that involved civil unrest were the result of ethnic hatred, a lack of civil authority, food shortages, a revolution, and religious-based fighting factions.

1-2. Civil unrest may range from simple, nonviolent protests that address specific issues, to events that turn into full-scale riots. Gathering in protest may be a recognized right of any person or group, regardless of where U.S. forces may be operating. In the United States, this fundamental right is protected under the *Constitution of the United States,* while other countries have various laws that protect the rights of their citizens rights. During unified action, U.S. forces should never violate basic civil or human rights. Most protesters are law-abiding citizens who intend to keep their protests nonviolent, but some protest planners insist that the event involve violence. Often in the media, protesters can gain sympathy for their cause by prompting authorities to take physical action against them. Violence can be the result of demonstrators beginning to conduct unlawful or criminal acts and authorities (who are responsible for the safety and welfare of all) enforcing the laws of the municipality, state, or nation. The level of violence is determined by the willingness of demonstrators to display and voice their opinions in support of their cause and the actions and reactions of the control force on scene.

1-3. Commanders must be aware of the possibility that some individuals or groups within an organized demonstration may intend to cause disruption, incite violence, destroy property, and provoke authorities. The situation and actions of the crowd may dictate control and enforcement options. Agitators and criminal infiltrators within the crowd can lead to the eruption of violence. Inciting a crowd to violence or a greater intensity of violence by using severe enforcement tactics must be avoided.

1-4. Community unrest results in urban conflicts that arise from highly emotional social and economic issues. Economically deprived residents may feel that they are treated unjustly or ignored by people in power and authority. Tensions can build quickly in a community over a variety of issues, such as hunger, poor employment opportunities, inadequate community services, poor housing, and labor issues. Tensions in these areas create the potential for violence. When tensions are high, it takes a small (seemingly minor) incident, rumor, or perceived act of injustice to ignite groups within a crowd to riot and act violently. This is particularly true if community relations with authorities are strained.

1-5. Significant ethnic differences in a community can create an atmosphere of distrust, even hatred. Unrest among ethnic groups competing for jobs, living areas, and sparse essentials can cause an eruption of civil disorder that can lead to full riots. As emotions run high, violence becomes likely.

1-6. Terrorist organizations may infiltrate groups within a demonstrating crowd. These terrorist groups may intend to embarrass their government or other governments. Terrorist infiltrators can be used to provoke crowds as a diversion, as part of a demonstration, or as cover for terrorist acts.

CROWD DEVELOPMENT

1-7. Crowds are a gathering of a multitude of individuals and small groups that have temporarily assembled in the same place. These small groups are usually composed of friends, family members, or acquaintances that represent a group belief or cause. People in small groups are known only to companions in their group and to others in the gathering that have come from the same neighborhood or community. Commanders must consider how the individuals and small groups assembled and how they are interacting during the gathering process. Crowd development is a process with a beginning, middle, and end.

> *Note.* During planning, leaders must consider that the crowd may become more combative with the arrival of a response force.

ASSEMBLY PROCESS

1-8. The first phase of crowd development is the assembly process. The assembly process of a gathering refers to the movement of people from different locations to a common location within a given period. This largely determines who participates.

1-9. Gatherings are often assisted by the activities of individuals or groups with a specific agenda, such as yelling catchy slogans and cheers that everyone can easily pick up and join in. Some groups are so well organized that they can prestage leaders to infiltrate a gathering. This creates unity, even inciting newcomers to join their cause. It can occur in one of two ways—impromptu or organized.

Impromptu

1-10. An impromptu assembly usually develops informally and is mostly done by word of mouth (one person to another or one group to another). Participants spread information by telling one another when, where, and what is happening and inviting them to participate. An example of an impromptu gathering would be a gathering at a secured food distribution point after receiving information (by word of mouth) that a large truck carrying much-needed supplies and food is about to arrive. In this case, hunger would be the driving force causing the migration of people to the food distribution point. A more recent way of establishing an informal gathering is by spreading information via electronic means (text messages or social media). Examples of this are best illustrated in Egypt and other countries during the Arab Spring that began in 2010 and in the United States during Occupy Wall Street that began in 2011.

Organized

1-11. Like an impromptu assembly, an organized assembly also involves individuals and groups passing on information to one another. Passing information on police activity and occurrences and when and where events will take place helps organizers to prestage participants. Rarely is only one group responsible for pulling together a gathering. Organized assemblies rely heavily on established groups that attract people to gather. Examples of well-organized groups are anarchists, antiglobalization groups, and antifree enterprise groups. Groups representing extreme religious faiths and ethnic organizations have been common as well. Another example of organized groups that contribute to the assembly process of certain gatherings is the labor unions. Labor unions played a large role in the 2011 Wisconsin protests that included passing on information and transporting participants.

1-12. Organized-gathering processes rely more on centralized planning and organization. One or more groups offer the organizers lists of individual names and groups from which they contact as potential participants. Modern technologies that allow for rapid information dissemination are available to these organizers. They can also use telephone banks, mailing lists, or e-mail addresses. In preparation for a long-term event, some group organizers have the means to provide logistical support, such as transportation, food, and water for the participants.

GATHERING

1-13. The second phase of crowd development is the gathering itself. Studies show that—
- Crowds are made of many entities and all participants are not the same.
- Crowds are not made of isolated individuals, but of a minority of individuals and a majority of small groups who may or may not be acquainted with each other.
- Groups and individuals in the crowd are not unanimous in their motivation.
- Groups and individuals in the crowd are usually not anonymous to each other, especially different groups who gathered at the same place.
- Individuals within a group do not want to draw specific attention to themselves and they do not participate in unique, emotional displays.
- Groups within a crowd will often act in unison in an attempt to achieve their agendas.
- Crowds are generally not unique or distinguished by violence or unlawful conduct.

DISPERSAL PROCESS

1-14. The final phase of any crowd development is the dispersal process. It involves the movement of people from the common location where they assembled to one or more alternate locations. The dispersal process ends the gathering or begins its decline. Dispersal can occur on a routine, emergency, or coerced basis.

Routine

1-15. Routine dispersal is when the crowd leaves on its own with no outside influence. The dispersal may be specified in advance and can be included in the assembly instructions given by the organizers of the event.

Emergency

1-16. An emergency dispersal occurs when people evacuate an area as a result of an unexpected crisis (fire, explosion, bomb threat, terrorist act). Individuals in such an emergency quickly recover from the initial shock and often find improvised ways of extricating themselves and their companions from the dangerous situation. Therefore, it is important that forces on the scene are careful not to confuse group dispersion from an attack or regrouping tactics.

Coercion

1-17. Coercion dispersal is caused by a use of force on some level. This is not necessarily the best way to disperse a crowd. The negotiated management of crowds is the preferred method and has proven to be highly successful in getting crowd organizers to police themselves especially if the demonstration or protest leaders are available and willing to participate.

CROWD DYNAMICS

1-18. Understanding crowds and the gathering process is important because they can be applied to crowd dynamics. Under most circumstances, gathered crowds are orderly and present few, if any, problems for authorities. Crowds consist of people who, although very motivated and passionate, are also subject to their own need for creature comforts. Rainy or cold weather has a way of disheartening all but a few individuals who are highly motivated and disciplined. If problems exist, they usually fall into the following three categories:

- **Public disorder.** During a public disorder, there is a basic breach of civic order. Individuals or small groups assemble often and have a tendency to disrupt normal order.
- **Public disturbance.** During a public disturbance, there is turmoil on top of the initial disruption. Individuals and groups assemble often and begin chanting, yelling, singing, and voicing individual or collective opinions.
- **Riot.** During a riot, one or more groups or individuals within a crowd threaten or act violently toward other people or property and create an extremely volatile environment.

1-19. Panic can erupt quickly, especially when crowds turn into mobs. Individuals within the mob can easily sense that their safety and well-being are at risk. This puts crowd members in a fight-or-flight situation. The use of riot control agents (RCAs) by authorities adds to the panic and confusion. Individuals in a mob may attempt to leave the area, and then they may find that there are no escape routes and the roads are blocked. This can often lead to violent physical attacks.

BEHAVIOR THEORIES

1-20. Understanding crowd dynamics and behavior is important during the planning process. Information about the demonstrators (who are the demonstrators, where are they gathering, why are they demonstrating, and what are their capabilities) is necessary for proper planning. When coupling the understanding of why crowds behave as they do with the known facts, a more detailed plan is achieved. With this information, contingencies can be put in place so that the control force is proactive instead of reactive. There are multiple theories on crowd behavior, two of which are discussed below.

CONTAGION

1-21. Emotional contagion is the most dramatic psychological factor of crowd dynamics. It provides the crowd with a temporary bond of psychological unity. Lasting long enough, this unity can push a simple organized crowd into a mob. Normal law and authority are rejected by the crowd as a whole under these conditions, increasing the potential for violence and panic to erupt.

1-22. Being part of a crowd has certain effects on different people. Contagion theory suggests that each individual in a crowd is susceptible to behaving in a way that is contrary to their normal behavior. Some reasons for these behaviors could include the following:

- Crowds provide individuals with a sense of anonymity. With so many others, an individual realizes that they are just another face in the crowd, giving a sense of invulnerability.
- Crowd and individual behaviors are impersonal by nature. A them-against-us attitude affords those within the crowd the ability to freely (without hesitation or reservation) be verbally abusive, throw objects, or attack anyone who gets in their way.
- Crowds provide individuals with the idea that their moral responsibilities have shifted from themselves as a person to the crowd as a whole. Large numbers of people often discourage individual behavior, and the urge to imitate individual within the crowd is strong. Individuals look to others around them for cues of what to do next, disregarding their own background and training. Often it is only the strong, well-disciplined person who can resist the prevailing crowd behavior.
- Crowd behavior influences the actions of the disorderly individuals of the crowd and the authorities who are tasked to control them.

TWO-CROWD

1-23. The two-crowd theory is based around the belief that at civil disturbance events there are two crowds present, one is civilians that have gathered (protesters, agitators, on-lookers) and the other is the uniformed personnel (control force, law enforcement officials). According to the two-crowd theory, the outbreak of violence is not due to aspects of the contagion theory, but instead due to the action, reaction, and counteraction of both crowds that are present, known as circular reaction.

1-24. According to this theory, the blame for violence must be shared between the gathered crowd and the control force. It states that the actions and reactions of the control force play a significant part in the levels of violence that occur and places the blame on law enforcement. Therefore, leaders and members of the control force must be fully aware of their actions, reactions, and behaviors and how they affect the gathered crowd and its participants' actions and behaviors.

1-25. The interaction between the two crowds can be described using the metaphor of a dance, complete with well understood rules of dance etiquette. The escalation of tension and the potential for violence begins when one side or the other violates these rules. Through the violation of the implicit rules of dance etiquette, one crowd or the other triggers entry of both into an ever-escalating cycle of action, reaction, and counteraction. Dependent on preexisting expectations and on the present response, escalation of tension and violence may ensue.

1-26. Along with the interaction of the two crowds, there are several factors to consider for a crowd management event that affect the escalation of tension and outbreak of violence. Acknowledging and understanding these factors can help predict outcomes of crowd events and, thus, aid in prior planning and decisionmaking on the scene. These factors are—

- **Official anticipation.** Official anticipation is the prediction of the occurrence of an event and eventual outcome by control force leadership before the event. An expectation of escalation is created through public pronouncements. Media reporting predictions by officials result in a self-fulfilling prophecy, wherein authorities bring about confrontation by anticipating violence where none was imminent and by overreacting to minor incidents, making them into major ones.
- **Political intervention and diplomatic restriction.** Political intervention or diplomatic restriction affects the tactics and strategies used by the control force by limiting the options available, or by dictating the choice of tactics. For example, in some countries where U.S. forces are deployed, the use of chemical irritants is restricted. These restrictions reduce the on-scene commander's options and crowd control arsenal.
- **Choice of strategy and tactics.** Tactical and strategic choice points should be clearly identifiable. Determine if tactical and strategic choices (for example, containment versus coercive dispersal) made at those points served to increase or decrease the potential for tension and violence.
- **Rogue responses.** Rogue responses are apparent random instances of hostility on either side that serve to spotlight marginal participants and spectators and increase tension within core participants. This behavior is considerably more aggressive than the behavior of others with similar responsibilities. (For example, a control force member strikes out with their riot baton hitting a demonstrator out of frustration or anger because of continuous verbal abuse while the rest of the control force remains calm in formation.) To qualify as rogue, less than 10 percent of the members or participants engage in this behavior during an event and engagement is clearly excessive.
- **Application (and misapplication) of nonlethal technology.** Focused use of NLW targeted on obvious offenders may decrease tension. Conversely, random and uncontrolled application, such as spraying a crowd composed of participants, media, spectators, and passersby with a chemical irritant may increase tension, may put focus on those involved, and may result in counterviolence.
- **Boundaries.** Drawing a line in the sand randomly creates an artificial boundary that either crowd becomes firmly invested in to the point that their defense or their breach becomes a matter they believe requires the use of force.
- **Illusion of communication.** The illusion of communication is when the control force operates as though instructions (an order to disperse) have been heard and understood, but individuals, groups, and crowds may not have heard or understood because of language barriers, garbled amplification, or inadequate projection.
- **Denigration and vilification.** Denigration and vilification are the dehumanizing and stereotyping of opposing crowds. The depersonalization of the opposing crowd leads to the

magnification of the sense of threat. (As in, the control force labeling all protestors as anarchists, or when demonstrators label all control force members as mindless followers of an oppressive government.)
- **Goldilocks principle.** This principle refers to how the degree of response to a past crowd management event by the control force was characterized as too hard or too soft by political operatives or the media. Future events result in an adjusted response that is either too hard or too soft instead of responding to the situation as directed by the commander's guidance, planning, ROE, and rules for the use of force (RUF).
- **Official perspective.** Official perspective is a variable that is also known as *military police knowledge, military police perception,* or *military police worldview*. This perspective reflects the filters applied in creating the definition of the situation upon which strategic and tactical decisions are made. It incorporates organizational culture, predispositions, and prejudices; personal stereotypes; perception of legitimacy; and commitment to protecting the freedom of expression and assembly. As such, it contributes to a self-fulfilling prophecy—by behaving according to their assumptions and expectations, the control force may create and contribute to the expected outcome. If the crowd is predicted to change into a violent mob and behaves accordingly, then the chances of a violent outcome are increased.

CROWD TYPES

1-27. Gaining an understanding of crowd dynamics and behaviors that cause individuals or groups to join together is every leader's responsibility. For the sake of description, crowds are identified as casual, sighting, agitated, and mob-like or riotous. Do not confuse motives inferred from the crowd actions with the description of the crowd type.

CASUAL

1-28. Casual crowds are identified as individuals or small groups with nothing in common to bind them together. If they have an agenda, it is their own. They arrive separately and leave separately. Casual crowds are made up of individuals or small groups occupying the same common place, such as a shopping mall where these individuals or small groups meet.

SIGHTING

1-29. Sighting crowds are similar to casual crowds with one additional element—an event. There are numerous events that cause people to come together as a crowd, such as; sporting events, fires and accidents, music concerts, labor strikes, demonstrations, and protests. Individuals or groups gather at these events for the same purpose. It is the event or one's curiosity that compels a sighting crowd to come together.

AGITATED

1-30. Agitated crowds are generally casual or sighting crowds with the addition of strong emotions expressed verbally. As more people within the crowd become emotionally involved, a sense of unity can develop, causing changes in the overall demeanor of the crowd. Yelling, screaming, crying, and profane name-calling are all associated with an agitated crowd.

MOB-LIKE OR RIOTOUS

1-31. Mobs have all the elements found in the first three types of crowds, with the addition of aggressive, physical and, sometimes, violent actions. Under these conditions, individuals within a crowd will often say and do things they usually would not. Extreme acts of violence and property damage are often a part of mob activities. Mobs consist of (or involve) the elements of people and groups being mixed together and becoming fluid.

CROWD TACTICS

1-32. During a civil disturbance, individuals and small groups within a crowd use any number of tactics to resist authority, disrupt, and add turmoil to achieve their goals. The more organized and purposeful a crowd becomes, the more likely that a tactic will be used. These tactics can be planned or unplanned and violent or nonviolent.

1-33. Commanders and leaders must be aware that highly organized groups of protesters and demonstrators have developed tactics to disrupt the control force. These crowd tactics were published in handbooks for communist organizers during the Cold War, and today, the Internet contains sites that are devoted to sharing these and other tactics with the general public and various protest groups. Although some of these tactics are outdated, commanders and leaders must be aware of them and their potential consequences. Commanders must be aware that well-organized crowds may attempt to engage the control force, surround it, and overpower it by sheer numbers. To avoid this, commanders must do a detailed terrain analysis (intelligence preparation of the battlefield [IPB]) of the area to include all approach and exit routes in the area. The control force flanks have to be protected to avoid being enveloped by the mob. To avoid being enveloped, the on-site commander should keep the crowd at a comfortable distance from the control force formation. Establishing predetermined rally points for the control force is critical in the event that this type of tactic is used by the crowd.

NONVIOLENT TACTICS

1-34. Most gatherings of individuals and small groups into a crowd do not involve violent behavior. A public disorder or disturbance usually involves some name-calling, demonstrations to express views, corporate yelling and chanting, and even singing and dancing. Nonviolent actions of a crowd are disruptive because they are in direct conflict with what authorities want them to do, such as refusing to leave when directed, locking arms, and sitting in front of or around areas and buildings that the authorities are attempting to clear.

VIOLENT TACTICS

1-35. A crowd that becomes a mob can be very violent and destructive. Although some nonviolent activities occur, violent crowds strike out physically at bystanders, others in the crowd, or members of the control force on the scene. They destroy private and government property, set fires, employ bombs (in extreme cases), or use other weapons or tools at their disposal. Some violent tactics, such as setting fires, are done to create confusion or as a diversion from another activity. The only limitations for violent crowds are their own imaginations, the training of their leaders, and the materials readily available.

1-36. Riots vary considerably in targets and players. A communal riot, for instance, deals with deep-seated ethnic, religious, and language differences. Commodity riots involve an attack on property by acts of vandalism, looting, and arson. Protest riots (such as the riot around the World Trade Organization Assembly in Seattle, Washington in 1999), illustrated individuals and groups that aggressively and sometimes violently acted out or voiced their opposition to the assembly. The Democratic Convention in Chicago, Illinois, in 1968 reflects a riot that directly targeted police and authority in general. Celebration riots occur across the United States as a result of home team victories in sporting events, among other reasons. Celebrating crowds look to make the moment more memorable through raucous acts that demonstrate their joy or happiness; for example, the riots that took place in Chicago in 1992 as a result of the Chicago Bulls winning the National Basketball Association Championship.

COMMON TACTICS USED AGAINST AUTHORITIES DURING A RIOT

1-37. Organized mobs try to defeat, disrupt, confuse, and deter the control force by employing several different tactics. These tactics include—
- Constructing barricades.
- Using weapons and projectiles.
- Feinting and flanking actions.
- Participating in verbal abuse.

Chapter 1

- Perceiving that people are innocent or weak.
- Using vehicles or other objects.
- Setting fires.

Barricades

1-38. Violent crowds may erect physical barriers to impede the movement and prevent authorities from entering certain areas or buildings to hide their activities. Common materials used for barricades include—
- Vehicles.
- Felled trees.
- Furniture.
- Felled light poles.
- Fencing materials.

1-39. By constructing barricades, the rioters are trying to disrupt the movement of the control force. If the control force does advance toward the barricade, the rioters want the obstacle to split the control force and leave it vulnerable to mob actions.

Weapons and Projectiles

1-40. Mobs will often use various types of weapons and projectiles against authorities to achieve their agendas and goals. It is extremely important that leaders train Soldiers to recognize possible threats of the various weapons that can be used by crowds or mobs, enabling the Soldiers to react with the appropriate minimum force. The types of weapons and projectiles used could be almost anything. Some examples include, but are not limited to—
- Firearms.
- Molotov cocktails.
- Explosives.
- Blades.
- Baseball bats.
- Axes.
- Bottles.
- Rocks.

1-41. Sniping or massing fire from within the crowd, in buildings, or other covered positions can, at times, be effective tools for terrorists or other belligerent rioters using a crowd to cover their acts.

1-42. Angry mobs will often attempt to disrupt the control force by throwing rocks and other projectiles. As the situation deteriorates, the mob may escalate the violence by using a battery of slingshots that will pellet the control force with projectiles. They may also use smoke grenades (homemade or store-bought) to mask their movements. Molotov cocktails are also used against personnel, employed vehicles, and portions of the control force. A group or individual may attempt to gain a position above an armored vehicle to enable them to drop a Molotov cocktail into an open hatch.

1-43. Explosives can be used by rioters in many ways: as simple diversions, to block the advances of formations, or to provide an escape for rioters. In worst-case scenarios, explosives can be used to purposely kill, injure, or demoralize authorities that are protecting the safety of everyone.

1-44. In many cases, a crowd throws anything in their reach that can be picked up. Rotten fruit or vegetables, rocks, bricks, bottles, sticks, and pieces of lumber are most often used because they are readily available. More sophisticated types of thrown objects are improvised bombs, such as petrol bombs or tennis balls with nails sticking out of them. Never discount that these individuals and groups could acquire hand-thrown explosives, such as dynamite or grenades.

Feinting and Flanking Actions

1-45. Organized mobs may attempt to disrupt the movement of the control force by feinting an assault. When the control force moves to blunt the assault, the mob will assault the exposed flanks in an attempt to split the control force and envelop a portion of it.

Verbal Abuse

1-46. In almost every instance of a civil disturbance or riot, verbal abuse will be an aggressive tool. Obscene language, racial remarks, taunts, ridicules, and jeers should always be expected. It is apparent that the purpose for using verbal abuse is to anger, demoralize, and provoke a physical response. Undisciplined, untrained Soldiers who face such an attack could cause the situation to escalate. Just one provoked action of a Soldier could be interpreted as an act of brutality by the media.

Perceived Innocent or Weak People

1-47. Women, children, and the elderly are often used as pawns in civil disturbance events. On many occasions, the innocent and the weak are moved to the front of the crowd and used as a barrier. With the innocent and the weak directly facing authorities, aggressive and violence-prone individuals or groups behind them attempt to provoke authorities to react. Often, this tactic is to exploit the situation in the eyes of the media for propaganda value. Despite the perception of sometimes being weaker, women, children, and the elderly can be just as committed to the cause as those behind them.

Vehicles and Other Objects

1-48. Vehicles and other objects can be placed on higher ground (atop a hill or in a building) to disrupt the control force. For example, a vehicle or tire can be set on fire and rolled down a hill, carts or barrels filled with hazardous or flammable materials can be pushed down a hill, or burning furniture and petrol bombs can be thrown from two-story or higher buildings toward a formation of Soldiers.

Fire

1-49. Rioters have set buildings, vehicles, and other structures on fire to block the advances of authorities and to create confusion and diversions. If property damage is the goal of a crowd, fire is an effective tool. A sniper, for example, may set a building on fire to divert attention or provide maximum target possibilities. Another tactic sometimes used is to flood the lower floors or basements of structures with flammable liquids or gas and then ignite it at an opportune moment.

This page intentionally left blank.

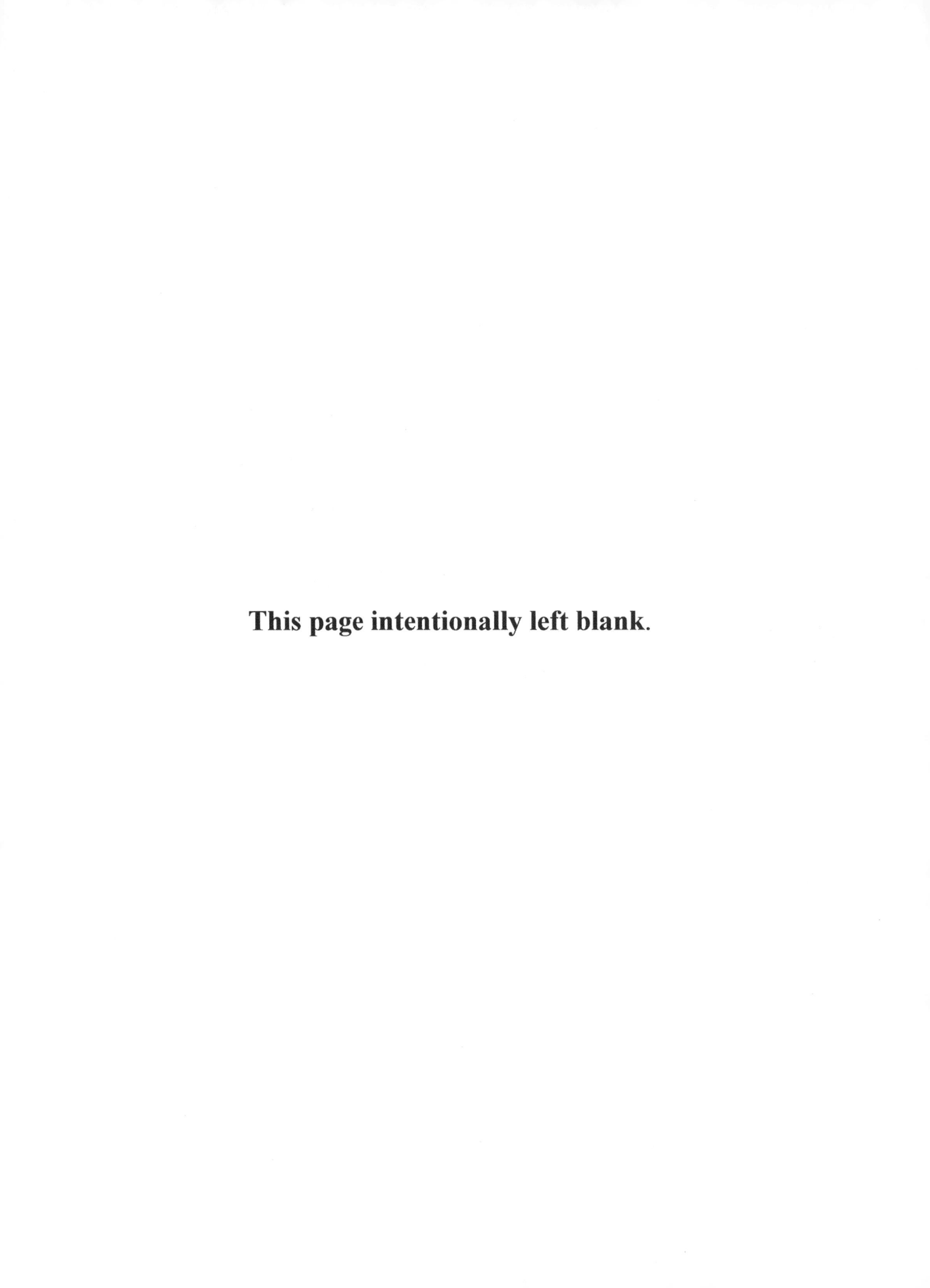

Chapter 2
Control Force Planning and Tactics

Crowd management requires its own thought process. Emphasis should be on prevention rather than confrontation. In combat, military forces are taught to fight and eliminate threats. In crowd control, military forces must deal with noncombatants that have recognized rights; these rights must be respected while maintaining public order. This is an issue that law enforcement agencies (LEAs) have been struggling with for years. Dealing with crowd control incidents is a matter of using some basic guidelines. It also includes asking the right questions in a logical manner so that key issues are not omitted. Commanders and staffs must use these guidelines along with mission variables (mission, enemy, terrain and weather, troops and support available, time available, and civil considerations [METT-TC]), the location of the incident (CONUS or OCONUS), and the risk management process (see FM 5-19) to ensure that proper planning and appropriate tactics are used.

PLANNING CONSIDERATIONS

2-1. Information is the key to developing civil disturbance plans. One must know who the demonstrators are; when, where, and why they are demonstrating; what their capabilities are; and what their possible course of action (COA) is. A commander's need for current, valid information cannot be overemphasized. The commander must learn as much as they can about the participants (their age range, motivations, strategies, tactics, targets, and dedication). The more knowledge that commanders have about the participants, the better equipped they are to counter different actions. Along with information on the situation itself, commanders and staffs need to know what they are authorized and prohibited from doing legally. Commanders and staffs need sound information, along with integrating risk management, to decide how to best use their available resources.

2-2. The side that possesses better information and uses that information to gain understanding has a major advantage over its opponent. Forces that have this advantage can use it to bring about changes in attitudes, decisions, and actions in assembled demonstrators. In planning for crowd control or civil disturbance missions, planners must decide what data is needed to develop threat assessments and courses of action.

LEGAL CONSIDERATIONS

2-3. Commanders must know the legal boundaries, their sources, and how they apply to interacting with civilians in OCONUS and CONUS. The staff judge advocate (SJA) office is able to assist with information as well. The SJA office should be included in planning and involved in any activity with potential legal implications. For civil disturbance missions there are differences in the legal boundaries, and in how U.S. federal forces can be utilized, depending on if the event is within the United States or within a foreign country. The planning and execution for these missions needs to be conducted within those legal parameters.

Continental United States Versus Outside the Continental United States

2-4. For the U.S. Army, conducting civil disturbance missions within the United States. will vary greatly when compared to conducting civil disturbance missions within a foreign country where the U.S. Army is conducting operations. Except as expressly authorized by the *Constitution of the United States* or by another act of Congress, the Posse Comitatus Act (18 USC 1385) prohibits the use of the Active Army as enforcement officials to execute state or federal law and perform direct law enforcement functions within

CONUS. For OCONUS operations, especially when the HN does not have a legitimate government or law enforcement capabilities, the U.S. Army may have to perform these functions, including responding to civil disturbances and performing the tactics and techniques discussed in this manual.

2-5. When the U.S. Army is conducting unified land operations within a foreign country, and there is a need for U.S. forces to conduct a civil disturbance mission, there are certain legal considerations that must be made. These considerations include (if applicable): United Nations or non-United Nations mandates, status-of-forces agreements, international laws, HN laws, the civil authorities (if functioning) of the foreign country, and ROE.

2-6. Within CONUS, military operations would fall under the defense support of civil authorities (see ADP 3-28 and ADRP 3-28). Military support to law enforcement is one of two categories: direct and indirect support. When authorized by the Secretary of Defense, federal military forces may provide indirect support to law enforcement agencies; but support is limited to logistical, transportation, and training assistance except when emergency authority applies. State and territorial governors can use state National Guard forces for direct support to civilian law enforcement; however, such use is a temporary expedient and must be in accordance with state laws (see ADP 3-28).

2-7. The *Constitution of the United States,* laws, regulations, policies, and other legal issues limit the use of federal military personnel in domestic support operations. Any Army involvement in civil disturbance operations involves many legal issues requiring comprehensive legal reviews. However, federal forces are authorized for use in civil disturbance operations under certain circumstances. The following references pertain to the use of federal forces within the United States, therefore; commanders, staffs, and leaders must be familiar with, and adhere to, the parameters within them—

- Insurrection Act (10 USC 333–334).
- Posse Comitatus Act (18 USC 1385).
- 32 CFR, Part 215.
- AR 381-10.
- DODD 3025.18.
- DODI 3025.21.
- NGR 500-1.

2-8. The *Constitution of the United States* provides two exceptions for which the Posse Comitatus Act does not apply. These exceptions are based upon the inherent right of the U.S. government to ensure the preservation of public order and to carrying out governmental operations within its territorial limits by force, if necessary. These two exceptions are—

- **Emergency authority.** A sudden and unexpected civil disturbance, disaster, or calamity may seriously endanger life and property and disrupt normal governmental functions to such an extent that local authorities cannot control the situation. At such times, the federal government may use military force to prevent the loss of life or wanton destruction of property and to restore government functions and public order. In these circumstances, federal military commanders have the authority, in extraordinary emergency circumstances where prior authorization by the President is impossible and duly constituted local authorities are unable to control the situation, to engage temporarily in activities that are necessary to quell large-scale, unexpected civil disturbances (see DODD 3025.18).
- **Protection of federal property and functions.** When the need for the protection of federal property or federal functions exists, and duly constituted local authorities are unable to, or decline to provide adequate protection, federal action, including the use of military forces, is authorized.

2-9. Laws passed by the U.S. congress include four exceptions to the Posse Comitatus Act. With the first three laws discussed below (10 USC 331–333) there is a prerequisite that the President must take personal

action, including the issuance of a proclamation calling upon insurgents to disperse and retire peaceably within a limited time. The four exceptions, based on law are—
- **10 USC 331.** When a state is unable to control domestic violence and they have requested federal assistance, the use of the militia or Armed Forces is authorized.
- **10 USC 332.** When ordinary enforcement means are unworkable due to unlawful obstructions or rebellion against the authority of the United States, use of the militia or Armed Forces is authorized.
- **10 USC 333.** When a state cannot or will not protect the constitutional rights of the citizens, due to domestic violence or conspiracy to hinder execution of State or Federal law, the use of the militia or Armed Forces is authorized.
- **House Joint Resolution 1292.** This resolution directs all departments of the U.S. government, upon request of the Secret Service, to assist in carrying out its statutory duties to protect government officials and major political candidates from physical harm.

Rules of Engagement and Rules for the Use of Force

2-10. The ROE are directives issued by competent military authority that delineate the circumstances and limitations under which U.S. forces will initiate and/or continue combat engagement with other forces encountered (JP 1-04). Clearly stated ROE are published before Army forces are committed. The highest military authority, with input from subordinate commanders, will continually evaluate the ROE and modify them as appropriate. Commanders must be aware that, in any confrontation ROE decisions made by Soldiers can have strategic political implications on current and future operations. Therefore, it is vital that leaders and Soldiers hold a common understanding of when, how, and to what degree force is to be used. This requires training.

2-11. RUF are directives issued to guide U.S. forces on the use of force during various operations. These directives may take the form of execute orders, deployment orders, memoranda of agreement, or plans (JP 3-28). The key with RUF is that the minimum force necessary to defeat the threat should be used. Force should be used as a last resort, and the use of force must be reasonable in intensity, duration, and magnitude based on the totality of the circumstances to counter the threat. (For further discussion on the use of force for law enforcement and security duties, see AR 190-14).

2-12. Commanders at all levels are responsible for establishing ROE and RUF for mission accomplishment that comply with the ROE and RUF of senior commanders, the law of armed conflict, and applicable international and domestic law. It is critical that commanders consult with their command judge advocates when establishing ROE and RUF (JP 3-28).

INFORMATION COLLECTION

2-13. Information superiority helps forces to anticipate problems and requirements. It allows commanders to control situations earlier and with less force, creating the conditions necessary to achieve the optimal end state. Inform and influence activities, military information support operations (MISO), and civil military operations are activities that may provide the commander with control techniques in the situational development phase.

2-14. Information is available from a multitude of sources. A diverse source pool is best because it prevents a single biased perspective. Primary sources are as follows:
- Open sources.
  - Libraries.
  - Periodicals and newspapers.
  - Television and radio.
  - Internet.
- Law enforcement sources.
  - Local LEAs.
  - National LEAs.
  - HN LEAs.

Chapter 2

- Military sources (according to AR 381-10).
  - Department of Defense (DOD) intelligence community.
  - Local military intelligence (MI) field offices.

2-15. Intelligence activities during the defense support of civil authorities within CONUS should be coordinated through higher headquarters for approval, in addition to consulting with a SJA. Additionally, Executive Order 12333 provides guidelines for the use of MI, including permitted and prohibited activities during the defense support of civil authorities operations (ADP 3-28).

Note. Most information collection activities are only done during operations OCONUS. The U.S. military does not conduct MISO within CONUS.

2-16. Police intelligence operations (PIO) is a military police function imbedded within the three military police disciplines (see FM 3-39). This function is a process of actively and passively collecting information that is of a police, criminal, or combat nature. As military police perform the three disciplines of security and mobility support, police operations, and detention operations, they are gathering information that supports, enhances, and contributes to the commander's protection program, situational understanding, and operational environment visualization by portraying relevant threat information that may affect operational and tactical environments. Appropriate procedures must be followed when providing police intelligence products to MI personnel with respect to American citizens or corporations. PIO can be a vital avenue for the collection of information pertaining to civil disturbances.

2-17. The IPB is a systematic process of analyzing and visualizing the portions of the mission variables of threat, terrain and weather, and civil considerations in a specific area of interest and for a specific mission. By applying IPB, commanders gain the information necessary to selectively apply and maximize operational effectiveness at critical points in time and space (FM 2-01.3). During the IPB process, the intelligence officer (S-2) or Assistant Chief of Staff, Intelligence (G-2) uses all available databases, intelligence sources, products, and related MI information to analyze the threat and the environment. The PIO function supports this process by providing the S-2 with collected police, criminal, and combat information that can directly and significantly contribute to the success of the MI effort. In addition to combat information, the PIO function provides additional information on possible criminal threats and COAs. This is intended to support the S-2 IPB process and can be used by the commander to upgrade force protection. When events have occurred that cause individuals and groups to gather into crowds, proper IPB (coupled with PIO) aids commanders in their decisionmaking process. Proper information collection, analysis, and use greatly assist the commanders in civil disturbance situations and help in the determination of control force size, placement, and tactics to be used. (For more information and regulatory guidance on information collection and acquisition, see AR 380-13 and DODD 5200.27.)

THREAT ANALYSIS AND CROWD ASSESSMENT

2-18. Threat analysis is vital for any military mission. The assessment of crowds requires its own set of questions. These questions should be answered before a crowd assembles or as quickly as possible. In some cases, all the questions may not be answered. The following questions represent a logical way to develop an understanding of the crowd the commander is tasked to control.

- **Who are they and what is the overarching identity of the crowd?** Do they identify themselves as strikers, ethnic groups, religious factions, social protesters, some other group, or even a combination of these? Understanding who they are will indicate what they may do. It may be possible to determine identities and goals from advance assembling instructions, leaflets distributed to bystanders, placards and banners, or chants and songs.
- **What are their goals?** What the group wants to accomplish by assembling could determine the extent to which they can be accommodated once they have assembled. They may only seek recognition for their cause (being seen and heard). If so, this goal is usually easy to accommodate. However, some groups may have more demanding goals, for example the demonstrators in Seattle who sought to stop the World Trade Organization. Goals that cannot be accommodated make confrontation very likely.

- **What is the composition of the crowd and are there any known factions?** Seattle demonstrations against the World Trade Organization were composed of groups that were protesting environmental issues, wages, and child labor laws. Differing goals and the resulting friction were evident between such organizations as the Ruckus Society and the American Federation of Labor-Congress of Industrial Organizations. Factions within a crowd represent threats and opportunities.
- **What are they capable of doing?** Protest groups often claim that they will assemble large numbers of people to produce some disruptive action. However, there is often a difference between the claim and reality. An organization may claim that it can mass a 100,000 people, but in reality can only get 40,000. Organizers exaggerate because they want to boost the morale of their own people and they want the media to report that they have strength in numbers. Studying the past activities of a group may provide indications of what they are capable of doing in the future.
- **What are their traditional behaviors or cultural repertoires?** What people do during protests is not universal. It varies with the group, individual, and the culture. Social protestors and striking unions may carry placards and banners, while other groups may protest in a quiet way. Understanding these behaviors, along with their goals, can be helpful in deciding how to respond.
- **When and where will they assemble?** Every protest organizer has a time and place for assembling and a destination for the crowd to move toward. If the organizer attempts to mobilize large numbers of participants, the time and place for assembling and dispersing must be made known in the instructions. This information may be stated in the mobilization instructions or disseminated by an informal network, such as word of mouth. Such impromptu networks in densely populated areas can enable rapid assembling. Knowing the location is a key to planning for a commander and their staff.
- **Where will they go?** Many crowds have destinations. Organizations may march a specified distance to ensure that their cause gets sufficient attention. Commanders need to know the route to minimize disruptions to the rest of the community. Knowing the route allows LEAs to take such measures as rerouting traffic to prevent congestion caused by protest marches. It is also necessary to provide security along the route to prevent counterdemonstrators from confronting the marchers. This will prevent an even greater problem for the community.
- **What are the possible targets of violence?** Riot participants, in particular, may focus on target facilities, personnel, or objects. There is no set target list for rioters, and it depends on the location and what is in the area. Some common targets include: authority figures (the control force), government facilities, food supply facilities, gun stores, retail stores (especially those with high value items), and symbols of authority or government (such as statues, flags, or signs).
- **When and where will they disperse?** Crowds have a life cycle that includes how they disperse (see chapter 1). Commanders must consider this. It is essential that there be one or more avenues that individuals and groups can use to disperse. These dispersal routes should be clearly marked, visible, and open-ended. There may be a need for U.S. forces to assist the crowd with dispersal. Assistance includes: securing routes, marking routes, and providing or helping arrange transportation.
- **Are there plans for subsequent gatherings?** Organizers may have multiple gatherings planned on different dates or locations. Also, a crowd may disperse for a short time so that participants can take care of personal needs. This could be days or only a few hours.
- **What is the worst-case scenario?** Worst-case scenarios must be recognized, discussed, and planned for, if for nothing else, to avoid them. This could be when an originally peaceful demonstration evolves into a full-blown riot.

PREINCIDENT PLANNING

2-19. Seek to know as much as possible about social protestors or other organized groups prior to a crowd management event. This will provide insight into the organization and its functions and provide a warning as to what to expect. Knowing as much about these organizations as possible, will help in anticipating their next move.

2-20. Preincident planning is initiated at the operational level with guidance from the strategic level. The planning includes guidance on crowd control and addresses responsibilities, training, organization, operating procedures, use of force and ROE. The most difficult and productive decisions are those made in the preincident planning process.

Define Goals

2-21. When defining a goal, determining the end state is one of the first steps. Defining the goal is fundamental. However, actually working toward and accomplishing the goal is easier said than done, as the process can drive the situation. Commanders and leaders must be aware of this. The military force must focus on what they are trying to accomplish.

Focus on Prevention

2-22. Planning should focus on the prevention of unfavorable outcomes. Experience has shown some LEAs attempting to help crowds accomplish their goals within the law has been beneficial and even led to conceding some violations for the purpose of avoiding confrontation. However, LEAs maintains a law enforcement presence, which signifies social restraint. The LEAs also decides when and where they will not compromise and the amount of force to use.

Avoid Confrontation

2-23. Crowd situations are highly unpredictable, but history has proven that confrontation will most likely cause crowd resistance. When pushed, people tend to resist opposition to the realization of their purposes.

ACCEPTABILITY

2-24. Deployed U.S. forces will find themselves engaged in crowd control missions under difficult circumstances. The host nation (HN) may have groups that do not accept the presence of U.S. forces, which will make imposing order and the protection of citizens difficult at best. U.S. forces will be under intense media and political scrutiny (an environment much like what LEAs operate in on a day-to-day basis).

2-25. Winning in this environment is not like winning in combat. U.S. forces may appear to be invincible and formidable, but they risk being portrayed as oppressors. Thus, U.S. forces can lose by appearing to win. Groups that perceive themselves as oppressed will readily seek being seen as victims in an effort to gain the support of public opinion. Winning in this environment is about seizing and holding the moral high ground. U.S. forces must maintain the authority and legitimacy of what they are doing.

2-26. Projecting a favorable image will require outreach to local leaders and citizens. It will also require developing a relationship with the media. For example, the Los Angeles Sheriff's Department often invites the media to accompany their tactical commander during crowd control situations. This shows that they have nothing to hide. It also provides an opportunity for individuals to see the commander's side of an event.

2-27. In this environment, commanders must consider how actions will play among several audiences—local, allied, United States, and international. The media effect is inescapable. In some cases, it will be difficult to accommodate all of these audiences. However, the most important audience is the American public, because it is vital to the continued support of U.S. forces.

RELATIONSHIP BUILDING WITH THE CROWD

2-28. Working relationships between commanders and protest group leaders are increasingly seen as the best means for preventing bad outcomes in crowd situations. This is called the negotiated management model of crowd control. The LEAs in large metropolitan cities in the United States and Europe practice it.

2-29. Open dialog helps develop working relationships between commanders and protest group leaders, providing an opportunity to communicate clearly. Talking allows group leaders to tell authorities and tactical commanders what they want to accomplish. It also allows authorities and commanders to tell group leaders what they are prepared to do and how they might respond to certain crowd behaviors. Such communications can do much to resolve issues and prevent violence.

2-30. Commanders may not be able to talk to all leaders before a crowd assembles. Some groups do not have recognized leaders and are ad hoc organizations. Other groups may have several leaders, but only some of those leaders will negotiate. In such cases, meetings with some leaders may tell who the other leaders are and provide critical information. Negotiations may also encourage more moderate leaders to do things that will support the commander.

2-31. Initiate communication with group leaders to work out issues before an event. Commanders should make a concentrated effort to maintain a working relationship with the leaders of protest groups.

2-32. Communication also means persuasion. Commanders should make a concerted effort to win over demonstration leaders. Commanders may tell group leaders that they want to help them complete their mission in a safe manner. They should encourage demonstrators to protest in an acceptable way. Several rules apply in negotiations, and credibility is vital. Only communicate necessary information and those actions that authorities and commanders intend to do. Negotiations are made from a position of strength, and by negotiating an agreement may be reached. However, contingencies should be developed in the event that the agreement is violated.

2-33. Working relationships between commanders and protest group leaders often result in protest groups policing themselves. This is one of the basic premises of negotiated management. Protesters are more likely to listen to their own leaders, as opposed to listening to U.S. forces. Protest organizers are likely to buy into a cooperative effort and agree to ground rules set during pre-protest negotiations. Many protest leaders seek to stay on the right side of the law.

WEAPON AND AMMUNITION CONFIGURATIONS

2-34. Individuals designated as nonlethal shooters must have the means to transition to lethal rounds, if lethal firing is required. Lethal rounds are carried separately from nonlethal rounds so that the shooter will not confuse them in the heat of confrontation. These nonlethal shooters must be well trained in transition drills from nonlethal to lethal firing, as well as weapons retention.

2-35. Squad leaders should designate nonlethal shooters within their squad. Ideally, the squad should not change its organization to accommodate NLW.

2-36. Commanders should not dispatch patrols with only NLW capabilities. They should plan patrols with nonlethal capabilities in addition to their lethal capabilities. Soldiers are never sent in harm's way without lethal protection. NLW are only considered additional tools for the mission and not a mission in itself.

2-37. Recovery, apprehension, and extraction teams should be established before deployment. Team members should be equipped with personal protective equipment, a sidearm, nonlethal munitions and weapons, and disposable restraints. They should have some training in open-hand control, pain compliance, and handcuffing techniques.

2-38. Crowd control formations (see chapter 4) should be well trained and well rehearsed. Rapid, coordinated movements of a well-trained and well-rehearsed control force can often be a strong deterrent.

2-39. Lethal overwatch, in the form of a designated marksman (DM), always covers the control force. During an engagement, the use of a DM provides confidence and safety to those facing a riot. The DM in an overwatch position scans the crowd to identify threats and designates personnel for recovery, as well as firing lethal rounds (if a lethal threat is presented). They are ideally suited for flank security and countersniper operations.

MILITARY WORKING DOG TEAMS

2-40. Military working dog (MWD) teams may be employed with a control force formation as a method of deterring the crowd from approaching or engaging the formation. The teams should be in the rear of the formation in plain sight of the crowd, but in front of the command element. The MWD teams work back and forth behind the formation as an intimidation measure. The presence of the MWD may produce a profound psychological effect on the crowd. These teams may also be used to help control individuals who are under the control of apprehension teams by acting as a deterrent to unlawful acts. (See ATTP 3-39.34 for additional information on MWD.)

> **CAUTION**
> Do not unleash an MWD on a crowd.

VIDEO AND PHOTOGRAPHY

2-41. Video and still camera men should make a photographic record of the civil disturbance scene, and especially individuals in the crowd who are leaders and instigators. Events must be documented to hold personnel, factions, gangs, or groups accountable for acts that violate law, destroy property, or cause physical harm. Electronically recording these events aids in the prosecution of such cases. Cameras also act as a deterrent since most individuals will not act in certain ways if they know they are being recorded.

URBAN TERRAIN ANALYSIS

2-42. Of all the environments in which the Army may need to conduct operations, the urban environment confronts commanders with a combination of difficulties rarely found in other environments. The distinct characteristics of the environment result from the combination of man-made features and supporting infrastructure superimposed on the existing natural terrain and the density of civilians in close proximity to combat forces. The human dimension it represents is potentially the most important and perplexing for commanders and their staffs to understand and evaluate. Commanders must make extraordinary efforts to assess and understand their particular urban environment to plan, prepare for, and execute effective civil disturbance operations. See FM 3-06 for detailed discussion of the urban environment and factors for planning military operations.

GRADUATED RESPONSE

2-43. The graduated-response process is a measured approach in response to a crowd gathering. By recognizing a use of force policy, Soldiers must be taught and understand that they use the minimum force necessary. Without the appearance of a graduated response, the gathering crowd may consider actions as excessive, causing a possible escalation of hostilities or violence. To aid in the graduated-response process, the following are possible actions:
- Try to persuade the crowd to quietly disperse by talking with leaders.
- Use translators as necessary.
- Let the first approach be by the local authorities (the mayor or police).
- Pass out handbills requesting that the crowd return home.
- Use video and still cameras to photograph individuals and events (this can be a deterrent, being used later as evidence).
- Give warnings before moving to the next level of force.

2-44. Ideally, the force should be positioned out of sight of the crowd. Have the troops move into position with few shouted commands. For maximum effect on the crowd, have them form their formation decisively and professionally. To aid in the formation process, if properly authorized, do the following:
- Display force in a graduated manner (for example a helicopter, hardened vehicles, and Soldiers with weapons).
- Exploit the psychological effects of show of force.
- Demonstrate force (not on unarmed civilians).
- Escalate the MISO message.
- Highlight the target pointer.
- Demonstrate sniper precision strike capability.
- Employ riot control measures.

- Use nonlethal munitions.
- Use RCAs (tear gas, pepper spray) if approved.
- Move through the crowd using riot control formations and movement techniques (see chapter 4).
- Use the graduated-response matrix (GRM) (discussed below).

2-45. With the increased participation of U.S. forces in unified actions around the world, it accentuates the need to establish procedures for applying graduated military responses to situations that threaten these missions. Numerous GRMs and similar products exist throughout the military. These products graphically portray available responses in a graduated manner. The intent of these products is to give the on-scene commanders a list of options with which to control or defuse a situation before it gets out of hand. Most threats can be eliminated without loss of life or collateral damage by effectively applying the resources available (see figure 2-1 for an example of a GRM card).

Note. Remember there is a difference in the actions that can be taken by military forces within CONUS as compared to OCONUS.

Crowd Action	Nonlethal Response			
	Command Presence and MISO	*Show of Force*	*Demonstration of Force*	*Riot Control Means (if approved)*
Unarmed Civilians	• Ensure that the on-site commander of the tactical military information support operations team directs the broadcast of the dispersal proclamation and passes out handbills. • Escalate the tone of the dispersal proclamation from information to a warning force.	• Display force along with escalating the dispersal proclamation. • Display force in a graduated manner, such as a helicopter hovering over a crowd or Soldiers with charged weapons. • Exploit the psychological effect of a show of force.	• Do not demonstrate force toward unarmed civilians.	• Employ RCAs at the point of penetration. • Use MISO to exploit the psychological effect. • Move through the crowd using riot control formations and movement techniques.
Armed Civilians (Knives, Clubs)			• Display force along with escalating the dispersal proclamation. • Highlight the target pointer. • Demonstrate sniper precision strike capabilities.	
Armed Crowds and Military (Firearms)				• Do not use RCAs; they may escalate the situation.
Hostile intent and hostile act occurs by armed threat.			

Figure 2-1. Sample GRM card

Chapter 2

Crowd Control	Lethal Response			
	Sniper Response	*Small Arms Direct Fire*	*Aerial Fires*	*Indirect Fires*
Unarmed civilians	• Ensure that target leaders or troublemakers are targeted. • Use the minimum response necessary. • Exploit the psychological effect of an attack.	• Determine that sniper response is insufficient. • Consider demonstrating capabilities. • Exploit the psychological effect of a lethal response. • Escalate gradually, starting with a small caliber, single round and work up to a large caliber, automatic.	• Determine that small arms direct fire is ineffective. • Use the minimum response necessary. • Use a minimal precision strike initially; use subsequent fires based on the situation. • Exploit the psychological impact of each strike.	• Determine that air assets are unavailable or ineffective. • Use the minimum response necessary. • Ensure that the response is directed by the on-site commander.

Armed civilians (knives, clubs)			• Close air support and indirect fires must be authorized.
			• Consider requesting permission for use when—
			  ▪ All lesser means have been ineffective.
			  ▪ There are physical eyes on the target.
			  ▪ Proximity to civilians has been considered.
			  ▪ Prudent risk to friendly forces and evacuee's outweighs the prudent risk of collateral damage.	

Armed crowds and military (firearms)				
Legend: RCA riot control agent MISO military information support operations				

Figure 2-1. Sample GRM card (continued)

PLANNING A GRADUATED-RESPONSE MATRIX

2-46. The planning for and development of a GRM begins with the mission analysis portion of the military decision-making process. Some missions require U.S. forces to enforce treaties or accords to protect the lives of civilians in uncertain or hostile environments (such as noncombatant evacuation operations) or to provide large-scale humanitarian assistance. These missions require some sort of graduated-response criteria to maintain order and prevent uncertain environments from becoming hostile. The development of a GRM requires the following seven steps:

- Identify the need for a GRM.
- Establish a GRM development team.
- Develop targets.
- Coordinate staff functions.
- War-game.
- Receive command approval.
- Operate deliberately.

IDENTIFY THE NEED FOR A GRADUATED-RESPONSE MATRIX

2-47. Not all missions require a GRM. The decision to use a GRM requires careful consideration. Once it is agreed that a GRM is necessary, it requires guidance from the commander regarding the response options available. Determining the appropriate responses is based on the facts, assumptions, and limitations identified during mission analysis.

2-48. Planners (staff) must agree on the intent of the GRM. The GRM can be used as a training and rehearsal tool. It provides leaders with the most likely vignettes that can be incorporated into a COA analysis, predeployment training, and rehearsals. The GRM can also be used as a handy reference during situations that require graduated responses.

ESTABLISH A TEAM TO DEVELOP THE GRADUATED-RESPONSE MATRIX

2-49. Establish a GRM development team with a broad range of skills, knowledge, and professionalism. The following list of individuals makes up a typical GRM team:
- Provost marshal or senior military police advisor.
- Fire support element.
- Brigade legal officer.
- MISO representative.
- Land information warfare or inform and influence activities officer.

2-50. Since the GRM is designed to give commanders graduated options for dealing with hostile and nonhostile threats to the mission, this team composition allows for target selection, application of the ROE, and attack methods using both nonlethal and lethal means.

Develop Targets

2-51. The fire support element, in conjunction with the S-2 section, develops targets for lethal and nonlethal responses. In the case of stability operations, these targets are usually not the conventional specific point or piece of equipment on the ground. They are more situational than specific. The GRM identifies situations or acts that subordinate elements could face during the mission. The sample GRM in figure 2-1 shows three possible situations or acts that on-scene commanders could expect to encounter. From the targeting standpoint, these are groups of more specific targets.

2-52. During mission analysis, the fire support officer identifies both lethal and nonlethal assets available to the unit. A tactical military information support team attached to the unit is an example of a nonlethal attack asset that should not be overlooked. The following are examples of what the fire support officer should look for:
- RCAs.
- Tactical military information support teams.
- Electronic warfare assets.
- Civil Affairs teams.
- Inform and influence activities.
- Artillery smoke projectiles.
- Aircraft.
- Mortars.

Note. Figure 2-1 is only a sample GRM card and would not be appropriate for every situation of civil disturbance. There are also significant differences in actions that can be taken by military forces when operating OCONUS as compared to CONUS.

2-53. The lethal assets described could be used in a nonlethal show of force or demonstration to defuse a situation before it requires lethal force. The critical element of this mission analysis is not to focus solely on lethal assets. In stability tasks, the Army wants to prevent acts of hostility first and then be prepared, if necessary, to apply lethal force.

2-54. Graduated responses can range from command presence through the show of force, a demonstration, the use of RCAs, and other techniques (such as the application of lethal force using snipers, small arms, aircraft, and indirect fires).

Chapter 2

Coordinate Staff Functions

2-55. To coordinate staff functions, the rest of the GRM team assembles to complete the escalation sequence for each response. Inform and influence activity and legal representatives are critical attendees during the escalation sequencing process. In the area of MISO, the tactical military information support team must exploit the effects of all responses.

2-56. The legal officer evaluates each escalation of force option and graduated response to ensure that it is consistent with the ROE. The GRM is designed to recommend applications of force consistent with the ROE, yet not limit the leader or Soldier's right to self-defense. A GRM should clearly show that if a hostile act occurs, a lethal response is an option.

War-Game

2-57. Once the types of escalations for each potential graduated response are determined and annotated, the GRM must then be war-gamed. The staff must walk through each act or situation from the on-scene commander's standpoint.

Receive Command Approval

2-58. Once the GRM has been war-gamed, it must be submitted to the commander for approval. This is the final check to ensure that the GRM team has applied the commander's guidance correctly and met his intent.

Operate Deliberately

2-59. Operating deliberately affords commanders ample opportunity to plan and prepare for possible civil disorder situations. Through the effective gathering of information and a working cooperation with local government and police officials, commanders can often be made aware of dates, times, locations, and what groups may assemble before the operation. The purpose is to gather as much information as possible: who is involved, where they are assembling, what incident promoted the activity, and what seems to be the prevailing attitude of the assembling crowd.

2-60. Civil disturbances are dynamic, ever-changing environments requiring effective communications both up and down the chains of command. They require advance preparation and planning using the established troop leading procedures. Troop leading procedures aid commanders and their subordinate leaders in planning and preparing for an operation (see ADRP 5-0). Most steps can be accomplished concurrently, but rarely is there enough time to go through each step in detail. Despite this, leaders must follow the troop leading procedure steps to ensure that nothing is left out of the planning process.

NONLETHAL WEAPONS

2-61. U.S. forces regularly perform peacekeeping and peace enforcement missions at a greater tempo than in the past. In the peacekeeping and peace enforcement environment, the use of conventional firearms or the threat of their use may not be the solution to a situation where U.S. forces must separate two belligerent, hostile ethnic groups or prevent a similar group from entering an area that is off-limits to them. However, a show of force using NLW and nonlethal munitions should cause crowds to disperse, separate, or leave the area with minimal casualties. For more information on the tactical use of NLW see FM 3-22.40.

2-62. The fundamental principles of mission planning are not changed by the incorporation of NLW into a plan. NLW are intended to be operational enhancement tools. The first concern of a commander is the successful completion of the mission. Nonlethal munitions provide a commander with a wider range of response options, but these munitions are not a replacement for lethal capabilities. Commanders must always be capable of answering a lethal attack with a lethal response.

2-63. When a commander commits their Soldiers and equipment to a crowd control situation, he commits his forces with the additional tools of nonlethal capabilities. This is an addition to the force continuum that the control force commander now has available. Commanders that properly employ nonlethal munitions and weapons have a tactical advantage over those who rely completely on lethal means.

2-64. There are various nonlethal capabilities, NLW, and nonlethal munitions available to U.S. forces. For more information on nonlethal munitions, capabilities, and training see TC 3-19.5. Examples of nonlethal include—

- RCAs (tear gas and pepper spray).
- Rubber and bean bag style munitions (fired from shotguns and grenade launchers).
- Riot batons and riot shields.
- Riot megaphone and other acoustical devices.
- Riot grenades (rubber pellet filled or flash-bang).
- Smoke grenades.
- Electro-muscular disruption (TASER®).

2-65. If the tactical situation dictates a nonlethal response, a Soldier who levels a weapon loaded with nonlethal munitions must be trained in distance to the target and appropriate points of aim. Based on the Soldier's understanding and training on the characteristics and capabilities of the round, they can easily discern and engage targets to the desired effect. NLW are only nonlethal when fired within their parameters.

2-66. Nonlethal munitions and equipment are not completely nonlethal; they are nonlethal by design. The term nonlethal does not guarantee zero mortality or nonpermanent damage. NLW can add flexibility to combat operations and enhance protection by providing an environment in which friendly troops can engage threatening targets with a reduced risk of noncombatant casualties and collateral damage.

> **DANGER**
> If NLW are fired outside their parameters, they may cause serious injury or death.

CORE CAPABILITIES

2-67. Core capabilities are those fundamental competencies that enable the commander to achieve the desired operational outcome. In the case of NLW, this includes providing a flexible means of response to protect friendly forces and influence the actions of potential adversaries and noncombatants. With nonlethal capabilities, these goals can be achieved without resorting to lethal force and in a manner that will minimize collateral damage. The core capabilities associated with nonlethal effects fall into the following two major categories:

- **Counterpersonnel.** Nonlethal counterpersonnel capabilities enable the application of military force with a reduced risk of fatalities or serious casualties among noncombatants or, in some instances, among enemy forces. There are several specific nonlethal counterpersonnel capabilities to be explored. These include the means to influence the behavior and activities of a potentially hostile crowd, and the capability to bring a mob engaged in a riot under control. While there are many similarities in these two scenarios, each involves unique challenges, which may require radically different solutions.
- **Countermaterial.** Nonlethal countermaterial capabilities enhance missions by rendering equipment and facilities unusable without complete destruction. Nonlethal countermaterial capabilities enable the application of military force to defuse potentially volatile situations under circumstances in which more destructive conventional military means might prove counterproductive.

NONLETHAL WEAPON CAPABILITIES IN FORMATIONS

2-68. The mix of NLW within the control force formation is based on METT-TC. For example, the first rank of the formation will have riot shields, riot batons, and their personal weapon (slung across their back [left to right] with the butt up and muzzle down or holstered). The second row will have a mix of shotguns and grenade launchers. Shotguns and grenade launchers may be used as area denial or point target weapons depending on the specific munitions used. The shotgun provides cover for the slower loading grenade launcher. The commander may move these weapons within the formation to meet the needs of the mission and to create distance between the formation and the crowd.

CROWD MANAGEMENT TACTICS

2-69. When operating in an environment where civil disturbances occur, commanders must be aware of the various tactics that are used in managing a crowd. Sometimes there is ample time for planning and preparing, especially if there is a scheduled demonstration coming up, and there is also good communication with protest leaders. Other times, a civil disturbance may erupt without any prior warning, and the response is conducted in a hasty manner. (See table 2-1 for crowd management techniques used during different levels of escalation and crowd behavior.)

Table 2-1. Escalating situation crowd management techniques

Situation	Response
Lawful assembly Lawfully protected activities • Speeches • Marches • Demonstrations • Rallies • Picketing • Public assemblies • Protests • Celebratory events	**Crowd management techniques** • Meet with event organizers and stakeholders • Determine crowd history and risk • Check permit limitations • Observe and assess crowd behavior • Separate opposing factions • Maintain a video log • Interact with organizers and gain cooperation • Use facilitation, not confrontation • Provide direction and expectations at mission briefing
Isolated unlawful behavior Isolated unlawful activity by individuals or small groups should not cause the declaration that the assembly is unlawful. • Isolated destruction of property • Isolated acts of violence • Isolated object (rocks, bottles) throwing • Individual sit down demonstrators	**Crowd intervention techniques** • Use organizers to gain voluntary compliance • Isolate, apprehend, and remove law violators as quickly as possible • Video Soldier and violator actions • Use amplified communication equipment to gain compliance • Use low-profile tactics, do not increase tensions by unnecessary aggressive appearance or behavior
Unlawful Assembly Assemblies may be dispersed when they are violent, pose a clear danger of violence, or when they are breaking another law in the process. Action may be taken to stop a crime before giving an order to disperse.	**Use Crowd Control Techniques** • Put control force in place • Identify dispersal routes • Use amplified communication to give dispersal proclamation • Disperse unlawful crowd • Video actions of Soldiers and violators • Apprehend those who fail to disperse or those conducting illegal activity • Ensure proper escalation of force • Deploy nonlethal munitions as needed to defend control force or to disperse the crowd

Table 2-1. Escalating situation crowd management techniques (continued)

Situation	Response
Riot One or more groups or individuals that are part of a larger crowd that involves threats or actual acts of violence against persons or property.	**Use Crowd Control Techniques** • Put control force in place • Stop the illegal activity • Video actions of Soldiers and violators • Apprehend law violators • Deploy nonlethal munitions as needed to defend control force or to disperse the crowd • Use lethal munitions if deadly threat exists • Ensure proper escalation of force • Protect lives, property, vital facilities • Remain present, reassess situation • Return to normalcy • Act quickly

Note. The civil disturbance response activities depicted in table 2-1 are carried out by the forces responding to the particular civil disturbance. Not all of these activities will be conducted by U.S. forces, especially if the event is within CONUS and federal forces have been authorized to be used in a supporting role. Legal considerations must be adhered to, and federal forces must follow all applicable laws and regulations. However, when the U.S. Army is the primary force responding to a civil disturbance within the foreign country they are operating in (OCONUS), U.S. forces may have to conduct most, if not all of the activities discussed in table 2-1. The following tactics would most likely be conducted during civil disturbance missions OCONUS when the host nation has no legitimate law enforcement capabilities and U.S. forces are in the lead. There are significant restrictions for the use of federal forces within CONUS.

CONDUCT HASTY MISSIONS

2-70. Conducting hasty missions seems to be the norm rather than the exception. Unlike deliberate missions, hasty crowd management is reactionary in nature with little or no time for planning. In these situations, the event of a crowd gathering is already underway. There is very little, if any, advanced warning of the unfolding situation, and commanders are usually put in the position of sending their Soldiers into an already volatile, and perhaps hostile, environment.

2-71. Commanders should be in immediate and constant communication with local civil and police authorities. The purpose is to gather as much information as possible about who is involved, where they are assembling, what incident promoted the activity, and what seems to be the prevailing attitude of the assembling crowd.

2-72. It is essential that commanders operating in environments where civil disturbances are likely ensure that their Soldiers receive training at all levels. Commanders and subordinate leaders need to instinctively rely on the same troop leading procedures that they would in a deliberate operation.

CONDUCT TACTICAL OPTIONS

2-73. In the peacekeeping and peace enforcement environment, the use of conventional firearms or the threat of their use may not be the solution. In a situation where U.S. forces must separate two belligerent, hostile ethnic groups or prevent a similar group from entering an area that is off limits to them, there are different tactical options.

2-74. Crowd control options are often combined. Commanders choose their options based on an evaluation of the particular crowd. Commanders select any combination of control techniques and force options they think will influence the particular situation (METT-TC). Commanders must always try to choose the response that can be expected to reduce the intensity of the situation.

Chapter 2

Observing

2-75. Observing an assembled crowd consists of gathering necessary information and watching them to determine progress and development. It is this gathered information that helps commanders select the appropriate actions. Gathered information can often be used to help defuse a situation through persuasion.

2-76. Observing is continuous. Without timely information, responses could cause the situation to escalate beyond what it should have or cause a response to be inadequate based on the situation.

2-77. Commanders may task teams with specific missions to observe crowd activity and note any new developments. Observing done by these teams gives the commander up-to-the-minute information so that they can gauge crowd activity and intent in relation to the overall situation.

2-78. Marksman/observer teams watch crowd activities and gather information. They observe and report on crowd size, location, and mood, as well as the developing situation. A marksman/observer team consists of a marksman, a radio operator, and an observer equipped with binoculars. They may be posted strategically on rooftops and other high terrain that overlooks the crowd.

2-79. Observing is also done through the use of electronic surveillance equipment. These camera devices are strategically placed to observe sensitive areas such as entry control points, perimeters, government facilities, as well as other important locations such as combat outposts. High powered cameras mounted on towers and aerial vehicles are important tools for observing and developing situations on the ground.

2-80. The timely flow of information may allow the commander to influence the outcome of the situation with simple negotiations. Observing is appropriate when more decisive action is not feasible because of crowd size or when the intensity of a situation might escalate. It is particularly useful in large, nonviolent demonstrations. Observing can serve as an interim measure until more control forces arrive.

2-81. Communication with crowd leaders and participants can help a commander control a situation without more severe measures. If communications exist with crowd leaders, the authorities may be able to divert the leaders or the crowd from their stated or apparent goal. Pressure can be put on leaders to channel the crowd into an area that minimizes disruption to the community and aids crowd control operations. March routes and demonstration areas can be limited to those that will help contain the crowd and reduce their potential for disrupting the community. Pressure can be positive (offering concessions) or negative (with deterrents).

2-82. If the commander can gain the cooperation of crowd leaders, it can decrease the potential for disorder. If crowd leaders seek cooperation from authorities, officials should try to be accommodating. Crowd leaders can be placed in liaison positions between the crowd and the control force. Crowd leaders can be made responsible for managing the crowd by policing their own activities.

2-83. Taking still pictures or videotaping the faces of individuals within a crowd may prevent or reduce unlawful and violent acts. If needed, photographs or videotapes can be used as evidence for prosecution. To be effective, crowd members must see their presence and actions being recorded. The photographer or camera operator should be in uniform so that the crowd knows who he is. Recorders must be close enough to the crowd to be seen easily, but not close enough to be endangered.

Blocking

2-84. It is not uncommon for protests and demonstrations against the United States or its forces to occur outside the main entrances to United States military installations or embassies. Because of the sensitive nature of equipment and information that can be found at these locations, blocking unauthorized entry is critical. Blocking is also necessary to stop a crowd from gaining access to sensitive locations, such as food distribution points, or other areas deemed off limits to unauthorized persons.

2-85. Blocking is the physical denial of advance upon a facility or an area by a crowd. Commanders may have to task their forces to block a crowd. Blocking physically denies crowd advance. Crowd control formations, particularly line formations, along with barricades can be used to block advancing crowds. Various items can be used as barricades to block (or channel movement) of a crowd. These items include: vehicles, concertina wire or other fencing material, concrete barriers, or other types of barriers like water filled barrels.

Dispersing

2-86. Dispersing is taking deliberate actions to fragment an assembled crowd to prevent the destruction of property or prevent injury. It is extremely effective against smaller crowds in congested urban environments. However, this may increase and spread lawless activity rather than reduce it. Thus, the commander's forces must control dispersal routes and the areas in which the dispersal will occur. Forces must protect the facilities that could be considered likely targets of opportunity for dispersing individuals or groups. Dispersal of the crowd may require apprehension of small groups or individuals still active in the area. Proclamations, shows of force, crowd control formations, and RCAs can disperse crowds.

2-87. Avoid (if possible) the dispersion of crowds into wide-open areas because it gives the crowd the opportunity to grow rapidly in size. The direction of crowd movement is difficult to anticipate and channel.

2-88. Once the crowd has started to disperse, it may occasionally be necessary for the forces to advance, keeping the crowd on the move and in the right direction. To avoid panic, a crowd on the move should not be hurried. At no time should the crowd be cornered in a position where there is the perception of no escape. This invokes an acute stress response, and can possibly escalate violent activity.

2-89. Issuing a proclamation (see figure 2-2, page 2-18) can help disperse a crowd. Proclamations officially establish the illegal nature of crowd actions and put the populace on notice that the situation demands special measures. Proclamations prepare the people for the presence of military authority and it tends to inspire respect. Proclamations support law-abiding elements and psychologically bolster military forces trying to restore order. They also demonstrate the gravity of the situation to all concerned and are excellent ways to make a commander's intentions known to a crowd. It is also a good way to reduce crowd size in case direct action is needed. Commanders can make a verbal proclamation similar to the following statement: "In the name of the President of the United States, I command that you disperse and retire peaceably to your homes."

2-90. In making a proclamation, a commander may consider imposing a time limit. However, the situation may change, and not imposing a time limit leaves the commander free to choose other actions when he wants. A proclamation must be specific in its instruction.

2-91. If a time limit is stated, it must be a reasonable length of time for the crowd to comply with the instructions. When drafting a proclamation, the commander must consult closely with the SJA. He must use the simplest language possible to maximize the effects of the proclamation. If proclamations must be translated to a local language, the translation must be made with great care.

2-92. The commander at the scene may direct that a proclamation be issued over public address systems. The force of the words used in the proclamation must be gauged to the composition of the crowd. If the crowd consists of normally law-abiding citizens who are presently assembled to show disagreement with an existing situation, the proclamation requires less force. On the other hand, if the crowd consists of militant rioters, the proclamation requires more force. The text may take a number of forms, depending on the situation.

> *Note.* The control force must ensure that the crowd actually hears and understands any proclamation given, to avoid the illusion of communication.

2-93. A show of force is often a useful measure for dispersing a crowd. When troops arrive, the psychological impact of their arrival can be used. Soldiers can dismount from the helicopters, buses, or trucks in plain sight of the crowd, but they must be far enough away to prevent a provoked attack of thrown objects. The first echelon to dismount from the vehicle secures the surrounding area.

2-94. When small groups are scattered throughout a large disturbance area, a show of force can be made by marching troops conducting motor marches, conducting patrols, and setting up static posts. Sometimes marching well-equipped, highly disciplined Soldiers in view of a crowd may be all that is needed to convince them to disperse and retire peaceably. On the other hand, a show of force may attract people to an event. It may also provoke a nonviolent crowd into a violent confrontation. METT-TC and information collection contribute to the decision of what type of show of force is to be used to aid in crowd dispersal.

Chapter 2

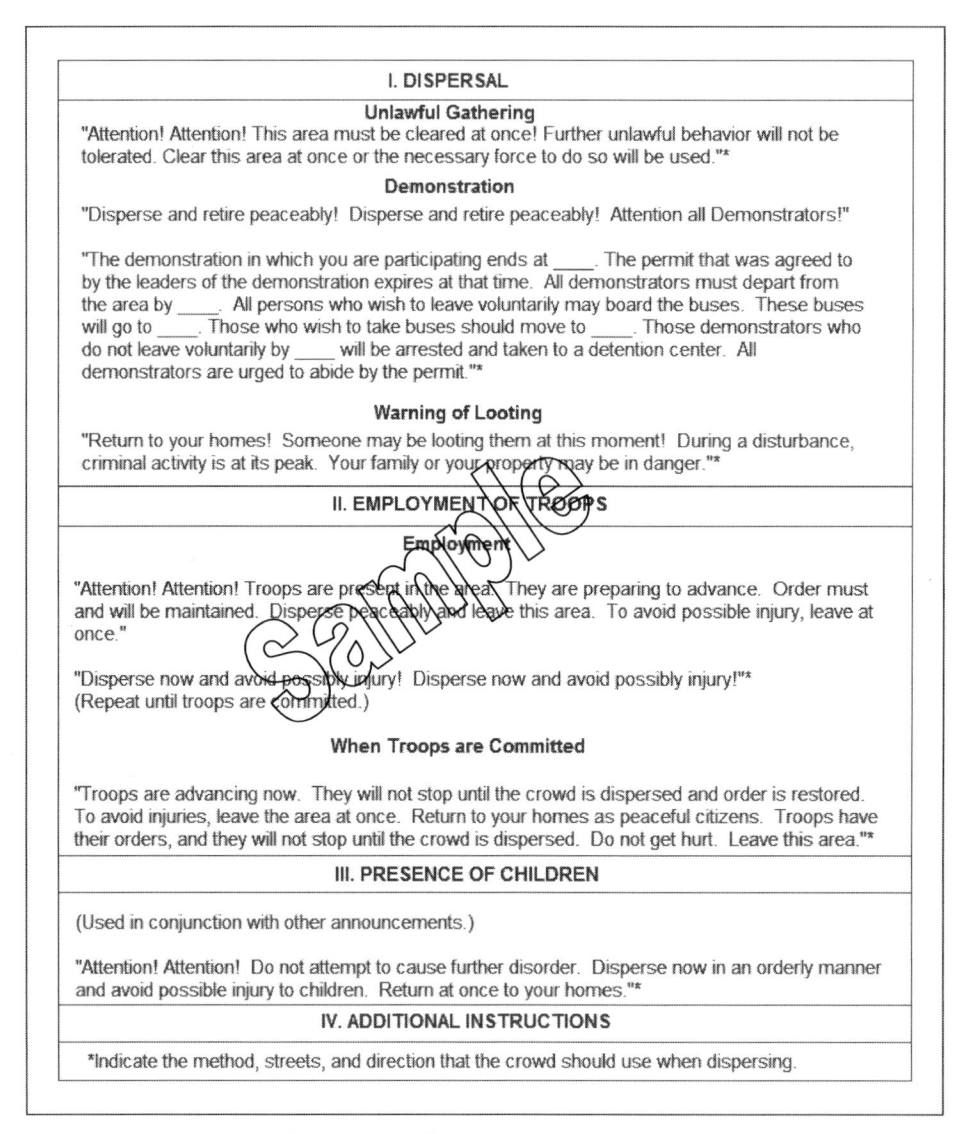

```
I. DISPERSAL
Unlawful Gathering
"Attention! Attention! This area must be cleared at once! Further unlawful behavior will not be tolerated. Clear this area at once or the necessary force to do so will be used."*

Demonstration
"Disperse and retire peaceably! Disperse and retire peaceably! Attention all Demonstrators!"

"The demonstration in which you are participating ends at ____. The permit that was agreed to by the leaders of the demonstration expires at that time. All demonstrators must depart from the area by ____. All persons who wish to leave voluntarily may board the buses. These buses will go to ____. Those who wish to take buses should move to ____. Those demonstrators who do not leave voluntarily by ____ will be arrested and taken to a detention center. All demonstrators are urged to abide by the permit."*

Warning of Looting
"Return to your homes! Someone may be looting them at this moment! During a disturbance, criminal activity is at its peak. Your family or your property may be in danger."*

II. EMPLOYMENT OF TROOPS
Employment
"Attention! Attention! Troops are present in the area. They are preparing to advance. Order must and will be maintained. Disperse peaceably and leave this area. To avoid possible injury, leave at once."

"Disperse now and avoid possibly injury! Disperse now and avoid possibly injury!"*
(Repeat until troops are committed.)

When Troops are Committed
"Troops are advancing now. They will not stop until the crowd is dispersed and order is restored. To avoid injuries, leave the area at once. Return to your homes as peaceful citizens. Troops have their orders, and they will not stop until the crowd is dispersed. Do not get hurt. Leave this area."*

III. PRESENCE OF CHILDREN
(Used in conjunction with other announcements.)

"Attention! Attention! Do not attempt to cause further disorder. Disperse now in an orderly manner and avoid possible injury to children. Return at once to your homes."*

IV. ADDITIONAL INSTRUCTIONS
*Indicate the method, streets, and direction that the crowd should use when dispersing.
```

Figure 2-2. Sample proclamation

Containing

2-95. Containment is the process of limiting a crowd to the area that they are presently occupying. It is a suitable option when the crowd must be prevented from spreading to surrounding areas and communities. Additionally, it prevents those outside the already assembled crowd from joining. Containment is useful when apprehensions become necessary. Containment prevents those in the crowd from escaping. Crowd control formations, perimeter patrols, and barriers are effective containment methods. In all instances, caution must be used to avoid the fight-or-flight response that is common to people feeling trapped with no escape.

2-96. Military vehicles are adaptable to roadblock operations as they can serve as barriers. They also provide added protection for the Soldiers inside and those outside manning the roadblocks because they provide an easily accessible barrier for them to crouch behind.

2-97. Military vehicles traveling at close intervals in a column formation next to a crowd are largely a psychological barrier (see chapter 4). They can be used to contain a large, fast-moving crowd. The moving cordon creates a temporary obstacle between the crowd and the line beyond which they will not be allowed to cross. A well-trained driver in a mobile cordon can do a better job than dismounted Soldiers. To execute safe, quick reversals of direction for mobile cordons on narrow roads, the Soldiers executing this formation must be highly-trained vehicle operators.

2-98. By-the-number commands issued over vehicle radios are the most common method for coordinating a cordon movement. Vehicles equipped with public address systems can also prove effective to issue both commands to troops and directives to the crowd. The cordon speed needs to be slow and safe, no more than 5 miles per hour with an interval of at least 20 feet. Blue and red lights, sirens, blinkers, and horns may or may not be used. Armored vehicles can also serve as mobile command posts. When used properly, vehicles provide security, communications, and mobility.

Patrolling

2-99. Alert, aggressive patrolling of the disturbance area deters the gathering of crowds. The use of patrolling is most effective for this purpose. It allows information to be collected, and it creates the psychological impression of the control force being everywhere at once.

2-100. Standard military transport vehicles provide mobility and communications for area coverage. Soldiers must be deployed with enough vehicles to provide the flexibility to handle all situations in the disturbance area. The vehicles can be modified with sandbags, wire screens, or similar materials to protect against sniper fire and thrown objects. Armored vehicles are used to help protect against sniper fire or other small arms attacks.

2-101. Armored vehicles patrolling an area of violence provide an added psychological effect and allow troops to maneuver close to snipers to make an apprehension. They may also be used as rescue vehicles to extract hostages or people surrounded by a hostile crowd.

2-102. Varying patrol routes and times for mounted and dismounted Soldiers keeps lawbreakers from being able to pick a safe place or time to act. Patrols are particularly useful in preventing overt arson and other acts of violence. Patrol members can also spot and promptly report fires. Whenever possible, military patrols are integrated with civil police patrols. Joint patrols conserve military forces and aid civilian military communications. They also help troops become familiar with an area quickly. In addition, the civil police are available to make apprehensions, if needed. Patrol members must practice proper standards of conduct and fair treatment of civilians at all times. They are performing an important community relation and control function.

2-103. Motorized patrols, because of their speed and mobility, provide timely reconnaissance and broad area coverage. Motorized patrols are always in radio contact with their headquarters. They can make periodic contact with foot patrols and stationary posts while patrolling their own areas. Moreover, motorized patrols can respond quickly to calls for help from other patrols and guard posts. Motorized patrols should have at least three vehicles with three personnel in each. Strength in numbers is necessary for protection. When planning patrol routes, avoid areas where the patrols can be isolated or placed in jeopardy. In addition, motorized patrols are equipped with fire extinguishers to put out small fires, thus reducing the burden on the fire department.

2-104. Besides foot and motorized patrols, air patrols provide a third dimension in directing the overall control effort in the disturbance area. They can perform reconnaissance and surveillance and provide near real-time information of the disturbance. They are an excellent means of providing timely information to the commander concerning the demonstration area and its surrounding perimeter. They can observe the actions of rioters, the extent of damage, the status of access routes, locations and conditions of road barriers, and other important conditions.

Delaying

2-105. Areas that units are assigned to patrol are often larger than the unit has resources to manage effectively. In addition, units must manage taskings, contingency plans, and other commitments, which will quickly drain available manpower. This problem will manifest itself when factions threaten to riot or gather in large numbers to demonstrate. In order for the commander to stall for time while they shift unit assets, delaying the arrival of buses and vehicles full of demonstrators is an option. This technique is based on the assumption that protestors are moving to the demonstration site by vehicle. Key and secondary routes into the demonstration site must be analyzed by the S-2 when they do the IPB.

Note. There should be an overwatch when this technique is attempted.

2-106. As demonstrator buses or other vehicles move toward the demonstration site, Soldiers in two vehicles block the road just ahead of the approaching vehicles. Once the demonstrators dismount their vehicles and begin to close in on the Soldiers, the Soldiers drive backwards approximately 1 kilometer (see figure 2-3) down the road to repeat the process again. This is repeated as often as necessary. This process, if repeated enough times, may discourage the demonstrators enough that they give up and go home. At a minimum, it provides enough time to shift assets to the demonstration site.

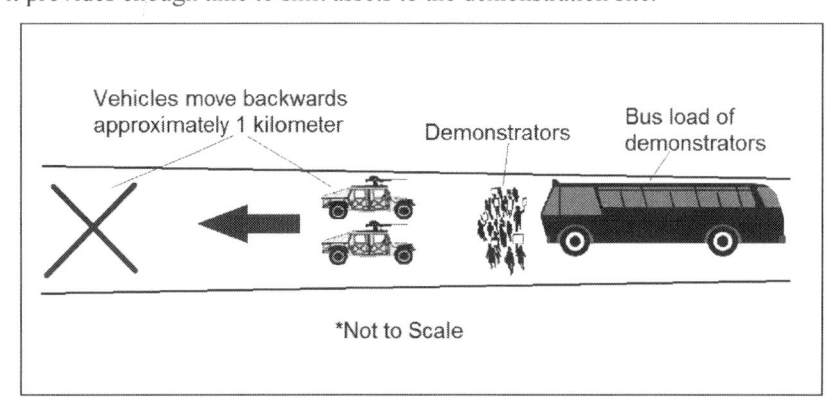

Figure 2-3. Delaying tactic

2-107. Demonstrators are just as capable of blocking areas or routes leading to a demonstration site. This prevents relief forces or other emergency services from assisting with the situation. One must remember that demonstrators are often well organized and have handheld radios and other items. A great example of this was the 1999 demonstration against the World Trade Organization in Seattle, Washington. Police had erected temporary portable fences in the downtown areas to keep demonstrators from disrupting the delegates. Determined to be disruptive, the demonstrators relocated the temporary fences, thus blocking police from that area. Police were forced to back patrol cars over their own fences to gain access.

APPREHENSION TEAMS

2-108. During the course of a civil disturbance, some members of the crowd may take part in unlawful activities, such as looting and assault. This will require the civil authorities or attached elements to apprehend, search, and detain people who are participating in the demonstration. Circumstances of the unfolding situation may require U.S. forces to be called upon to search, take custody of, and detain people who are participating in some form of protest and violating the law. Apprehensions are conducted to halt these violations and to deter future violations.

2-109. U.S. forces will be in a supporting role to the local civilian authorities or acting as the control force in civil disturbance missions. When making apprehensions, it is best to use apprehension teams. These teams provide quick, organized responses to developing situations. Teams can be organized at the team, squad, or platoon level depending on the number of apprehensions expected. Information collection and IPB help to prepare for events where apprehensions may be necessary.

2-110. Each team (if possible) consists of a civilian police or apprehension officer, security element, and recorder. Team apprehension officers make the actual apprehension with the help of the security elements. If there is not a civilian police officer available to act as the apprehension officer, then it will be done by U.S. forces personnel (preferably a noncommissioned officer or an officer).

Legal Considerations

2-111. All apprehensions are made by the civil police force, unless it is not possible for them to do so. Individuals must be known to have committed an illegal act, or there must be probable cause to believe that an individual committed such an act to be apprehended. If it becomes necessary for a military control force to apprehend or temporarily detain such violators, control force members often do so with the approval of the civil authorities. This ensures that all searches, apprehensions, and detentions (if necessary) are conducted within the parameters of the law.

2-112. Participating in a legal demonstration to express views is a right of all people, not just Americans in the United States. The actions, attitudes, and behaviors of U.S. Soldiers performing these operations are very important. Treat all people firmly, but with reasonable courtesy, dignity, and respect.

2-113. U.S forces should never be seen as a military policing force on our own soil or as an occupying force in another country. Treating people with contempt, hostility, or excessive force increases the likelihood of resistance and violence. Searching people, placing them under apprehension, and detaining them without probable and just cause or without concern for their rights creates problems and hinders due process. Numerous cases exist where authorities violated an individual's rights, resulting in the prosecution of police authorities or civil suits being waged against the officers and their leaders. This includes the military personnel assisting those officials.

2-114. It is very important that civil law enforcement (if available) is present and supervises all activities. Military personnel conducting a search or making an apprehension must carry out all the procedures carefully within the parameters of their training and the authority given to them. For each search and apprehension performed, the apprehension element must document the specific conduct of the person under apprehension.

2-115. Apprehending officers and supporting U.S. forces personnel must provide careful descriptive data for each subject. This description must be sufficient so that, at a later time, the suspected person can be clearly identified as the subject in question. Names and addresses of witnesses to the violation must be obtained. This information can be recorded on DD Form 2708 *(Pre-Trial/Post Trial Prisoner or Detained Person)*. Apprehension teams must retain and tag each item of physical evidence, such as weapons or stolen goods, which supports the apprehension on DA Form 4137 *(Evidence/Property Custody Document)*. The subject is provided a copy of the DA Form 4137 as a receipt for the collected evidence.

Apprehension of Subjects

2-116. Once an individual has been identified as a subject that violated the law, inform them that they are under apprehension. Ensure that the apprehension process is properly conducted and documented.

2-117. Security elements help the apprehension officer handle subjects. Security elements move, restrain, and search subjects under the supervision of the apprehension officer. The primary responsibility of the security elements is to watch the crowd and act as a blocking force, keeping the crowd from interfering with the apprehension. Recorders document the event, preferably by video, and complete DD Form 2708. If possible, recorders also photograph the apprehension officer with each subject. This aids in the identification process because it links the apprehension officer to the subject and provides the apprehension officer with documentation of the apprehension for use in court.

2-118. Electronically capturing the events as they unfold is essential in all civil disturbance missions. If personnel and equipment are available, videotape the events as they happen or, at a minimum, take still photographs to provide pictorial documentation that may be used later in court. Recording the scene before, during, and after the apprehension provides necessary evidence and can also help eliminate additional hostile and illegal activities. Having control force members take videos or pictures can help control crowd reaction and makes crowd members less prone to unruly or illegal acts. Subjects need to be transported from the area. In CONUS operations, civil authorities will usually be responsible for providing the transportation of a subject. Exceptions to this may be if the demonstration occurs on an installation. OCONUS operations may require U.S. forces to provide vehicles, such as trucks, buses, or sedans that will be used to transport a subject. Whenever possible, vehicles used to transport a subject should be modified with barriers to separate them from the drivers. If a barrier cannot be provided, a guard is to be placed in the vehicle. Passenger compartments are checked for items that could be used as weapons.

2-119. Whenever possible, female civil authorities or female Soldiers are to be used during search and transport of a female subject. If a female escort in not available, then a minimum of two males will be used.

Tactical Use of Apprehension Teams

2-120. During civil disturbance missions and the use of control force formations, apprehension teams are a great asset. Apprehension teams are not only stand alone teams used in apprehending subjects, but also can be part of an extraction team. Extraction teams are usually squad size and are generally formed from the support element. Extraction teams deploy from the control force formation into the crowd, usually no more than 10 meters, to extract individuals in danger or subjects to be detained. The control force protects the extraction team and provides immediate support.

2-121. Depending on the situation and METT-TC, apprehension teams can be used to move throughout the disturbance area primarily looking for law violators. If the risk is acceptable, these teams apprehend the violators. These teams are also used for information gathering and reporting, as well as deterrence to criminal activity from members of the crowd.

Chapter 3
Equipment and Techniques

During civil disturbance missions there are several key pieces of equipment that are recommended to enhance the effectiveness of Solider and to aid in their protection. Correct techniques and use of this equipment, along with proper risk management, aids in a successful mission by ensuring Soldier safety and proper use of force during civil disturbance missions.

RIOT SHIELD AND RIOT BATON

3-1. A Soldier may be required to be part of a riot control formation where their primary tool is a riot baton and their key protection is a riot shield. A riot baton is a very versatile weapon that can be used as an offensive or defensive weapon. The riot shield offers versatile protection, primarily covering from the top of the head to below the knees.

3-2. Use of the riot baton and riot shield is based on METT-TC and the commander's decision on use of force options. Formations committed to a riot with riot batons must have lethal overwatch, lethal and NLW within the formation, and reserve forces with additional nonlethal and lethal capabilities. The reserve forces are positioned to rapidly reinforce the control force formation.

3-3. During the termination phase of the disturbance (when the violence has subsided and is expected to remain that way), Soldiers are placed in a defensive posture. They may be equipped with a riot shield and a riot baton to perform their tasks. The riot baton is sometimes used as an offensive weapon when the formation is in close contact with rioters. The riot baton can also be used when formations are on the offensive and in contact with the crowd.

RIOT SHIELD

3-4. The riot shield has proven to be the first line of defense for a control force formation. The riot shield may also be used as an offensive weapon when in contact with an aggressive crowd.

3-5. The riot shield is constructed of hard, durable plastic and is held with one arm. It is secured to the support-side arm with a strap and handle system. This system is designed to make the riot shield an extension of the Soldier's arm. It is designed to protect the Soldier's face, torso, and upper legs. The riot shield is held at a slightly inward angle. This allows for debris thrown at the Soldier to fall harmlessly to the ground.

Carrying Positions

3-6. There are two basic riot shield carrying positions (see figure 3-1, page 3-2), they are as follows:
- **At-the-Ready.** The at-the-ready position is used while in a column formation or on the move toward a disturbance. This position is designed for rapid movement. It should not be used when in contact with a crowd.
- **On-Guard.** The on-guard position is used when the control force formation is in contact with the crowd or contact is eminent. It is used primarily in the following formations:
  - Line.
  - Wedge.
  - Echelon.
  - Diamond.
  - Circle.

Chapter 3

> *Note.* See chapter 4 for control force formations.

Figure 3-1. Riot shield positions

Defense and Retention Techniques

3-7. The riot shield is designed to withstand strikes from objects thrown by the crowd. Each riot shield holder must be confident in the defensive capabilities of the shield. They must also be trained and proficient in riot shield retention techniques.

3-8. When the control force is in contact with the crowd, rioting individuals may attempt to strip the riot shield from the Soldier. When a subject grabs the top of the riot shield (see figure 3-2), the riot shield holder slaps the riot shield with his strong hand near the subject's hands and gives a loud, verbal command "Let go, get back, get away, stop" while continuing to slap the shield until the subject lets go.

Figure 3-2. Riot shield retention (top grab attempt)

3-9. If the riot shield is grabbed from the bottom (see figure 3-3), then the riot shield holder drops to one knee, pinning the subject's fingers or hands to the ground. The Soldier gives a loud, verbal command (such as, "Let go") and stands back up. Repeat this as necessary until the subject has released of the shield.

Figure 3-3. Riot shield retention (bottom grab attempt)

RIOT BATON

3-10. A riot baton in the hands of a properly trained Soldier is a formidable weapon. However, it must be used in conjunction with other measures to be most effective. Soldiers must be trained with the riot baton to the point that its various techniques are automatic to them. This training must also include learning the vulnerable points of the human body so that they can avoid areas that may cause permanent injury or death when struck.

> **WARNING**
>
> **The riot baton is never raised above the head to strike a subject in a club fashion. Not only is it likely to cause severe injury, but it also gives an unfavorable image of the control force. The Soldier is also vulnerable to an attack on their rib cage when the arm is raised.**

Target Areas of the Human Body

3-11. The target areas of the human body are divided into three areas that represent the primary, secondary, and final target areas. These target areas (shown in figure 3-4, page 3-4) are represented in gray (primary), white (secondary), and patterned gray (final).

Primary Target Areas

3-12. The primary target areas are those areas, which when struck or restrained, because the least amount of trauma to the body. These include the meaty or muscular areas of the body, such as—
- Foot, shin, and instep.
- Inside and outside of the thigh.
- Lower abdominal region.
- Forearm and upper arm.

Chapter 3

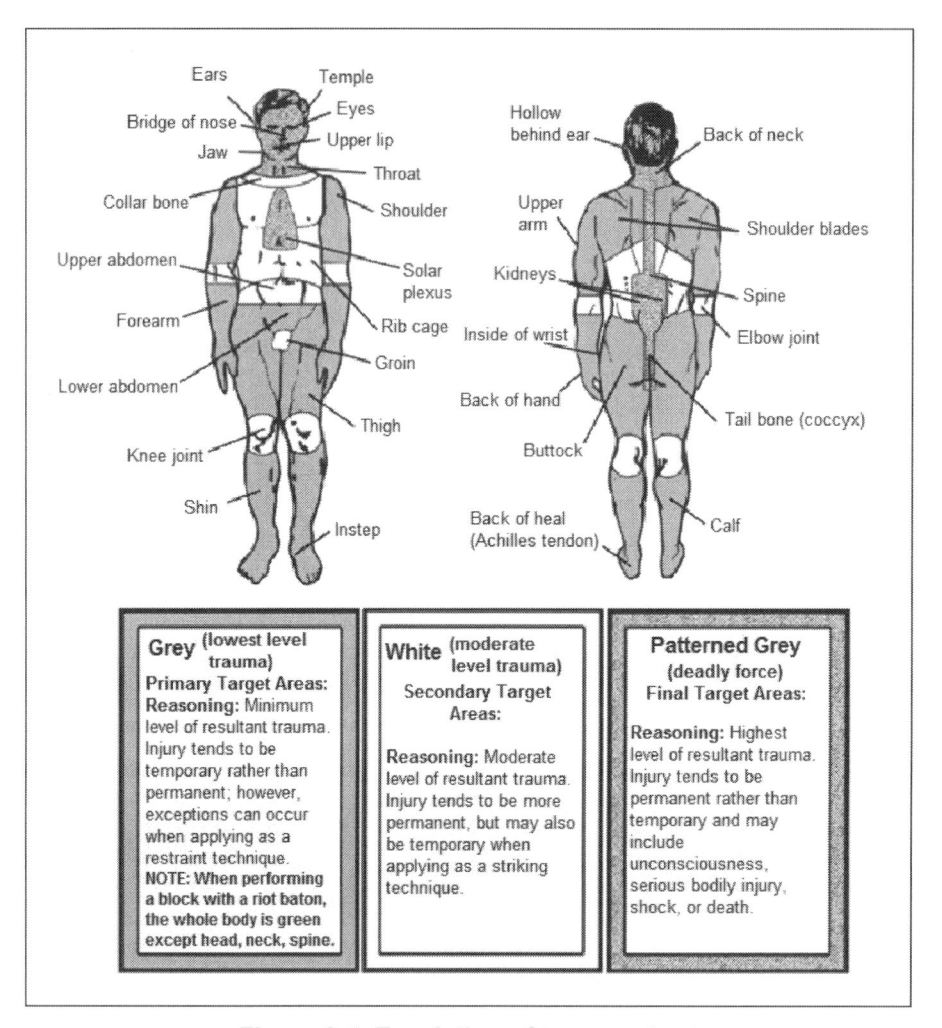

Figure 3-4. Escalation of trauma chart

Secondary Target Areas

3-13. The secondary target areas are those areas of the body, which when struck or restrained, cause a moderate level of trauma to the body. This type of trauma tends to be longer lasting because the time to heal is longer than with other parts of the body. If these areas are struck with a riot baton, serious injury may occur. However, some of these areas are used for control or restraining holds that tend to lessen the threat of injury. Some secondary targets of the body include—
- Collar bone and shoulder blades.
- Elbows and knees.
- Upper abdominal region.

Final Target Areas

3-14. The final target areas are those areas which, when struck with a riot baton, cause serious trauma that tends to be fatal or critical. However, there are some areas that (when used for restraining only), will not cause death or serious injury. Some final targets of the body include—
- Front and back of the head (eye, ear, nose, upper lip, and hollow behind the ear).
- Neck and throat.
- Upper chest.
- Xiphoid process (lowest segment of the human sternum).

- Spinal column.
- Groin area.

Types of Riot Batons

3-15. The Army has two basic types of riot batons: wooden and expandable. The wooden riot baton is approximately 36 inches in length and usually has a small, leather strap (thong) attached at the grip portion for better retention control. The expandable riot baton is 24 inches and expands to 36 inches. Regardless of the baton, all techniques for blocking and striking are identical. The riot baton offers offensive and defensive capabilities.

3-16. Soldiers must be properly trained in all blocking and striking techniques. Improper use of a riot baton by an untrained Soldier may have the potential to cause greater injury than intended to the aggressor or to the Soldier.

Parts of the Riot Baton

3-17. The riot baton is divided into four basic parts: the long end, long portion, grip portion, and grip end (see figure 3-5). Although the expandable and solid riot batons differ, their nomenclature is similar.

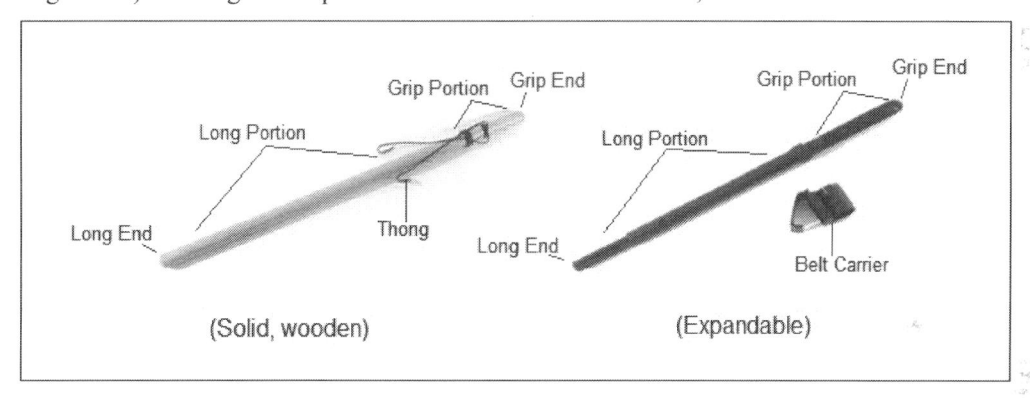

Figure 3-5. Riot batons

Carrying and Positions

3-18. As with any other weapon, there are certain carries and positions from which the riot baton may be used offensively or defensively.

Two-Hand Carry

3-19. The two-hand carry is intended for executing all blocks and returning with strikes. When the expandable riot baton is in the collapsed position (at 24 inches), the long end of the riot baton is angled downward approximately 45°. When it is extended to 36 inches, the long end is angled upward approximately 45°.

3-20. The Soldier grips the riot baton with both hands. The strong hand grips the grip end of the riot baton, and the support hand grips the long portion of the riot baton, 2 to 4 inches from the long end. The palm is down, with the strong hand pulled in close against the strong-side hip.

Outside-Arm Carry (Expandable Riot Baton Only)

3-21. The outside-arm carry is used with the expandable riot baton in the collapsed (24-inch) position only. Assuming a wide-based defensive stance (knees slightly bent and feet shoulder width apart), a Soldier draws the grip portion of the riot baton with his strong hand. Without striking out or widely swinging the riot baton, the Soldier brings the long portion up against the outer part of the strong arm (the tricep area). The Soldier's support hand should be raised in a position to protect and block strikes from an aggressor. It is from this carrying position that a Soldier can effectively use both the front and rear strikes.

Chapter 3

Vertical, High-Profile Carry

3-22. Assuming a wide-based defensive stance, the Soldier draws the riot baton with their strong hand by the grip portion. Once the riot baton has been drawn from the carrier, the Soldier swings the riot baton in a downward motion, fully extending the arm and holding the riot baton down and parallel to the strong-side leg ensuring that it is visible to crowd members. The Soldier's support hand is raised in a position to protect and block strikes from an aggressor (see figure 3-6). Although this carry can be used with both riot baton systems, it is best suited for the expandable riot baton collapsed to 24 inches. The vertical high-profile carry clearly shows the Soldier with a drawn riot baton in an effective defensive posture and ready for attack. A drawn riot baton in the hands of a trained Soldier may offer just the kind of deterrence needed to stop the activity of an aggressor.

Figure 3-6. Vertical, high-profile carry

Vertical, Low-Profile Carry

3-23. Assuming a wide-based defensive stance, the Soldier draws the riot baton with their strong hand by the grip portion. Once the riot baton has been drawn from the carrier, the Soldier swings the riot baton in a downward motion, fully extending the arm and holding the riot baton down and behind the strong-side leg. The Soldier's support-side hand is raised in a position to protect and block strikes from an aggressor (see figure 3-7). Although this carry can be used with both types of riot batons, it is best suited for the expandable riot baton collapsed to 24 inches. This position portrays the Soldier in an effective defensive position ready for an attack, but with a possible hidden weapon. In a low-profile carry, the Soldier holds the riot baton hidden behind the strong-side leg displaying a nonaggressive posture, while in a high-profile carry the baton is outside of the leg and easily seen. A drawn riot baton in the hands of a trained Soldier may offer the deterrence needed to stop the activity of an aggressor.

Figure 3-7. Vertical low profile

Riot Baton Blocking Techniques

3-24. The use of a riot baton in a defensive manner is done primarily through the use of blocking techniques. There are many ways that an aggressor attacks a control force Soldier. Common items used by the aggressor include sticks, baseball bats, bricks, clubs, and pipes.

High Block

3-25. The high block is very effective in blocking a downward, vertical strike directed at the top of the head and shoulders. This type of downward, vertical strike may be from a club, pipe, or similar object. The high block, is a three-step movement. To perform a high block the Soldier performs the following steps:
- **Step 1.** Raise the riot baton straight across the body until the baton is parallel to the ground (see figure 3-8, page 3-8).
- **Step 2.** Bring the riot baton straight up in front of body until the long portion of the riot baton is in front of the forehead (approximately 2 inches from the head). The riot baton should be in a horizontal position above the head and slightly angled down toward the support hand as it absorbs the shock from the strike (see figure 3-8). The fingers of the support hand should be open and behind the long portion of the riot baton when blocking the object to protect the fingers from being injured by the strike.
- **Step 3.** Assess the situation following a high block, and take appropriate follow-up action as needed.

Low Block

3-26. A low block is very effective in blocking an upward, vertical strike directed at the groin, lower abdomen, chest, or chin. This upward, vertical strike may be from an individual's foot, knee, fist, or from a weapon such as a club or pipe. To perform a low block, the Soldier performs the following steps:
- **Step 1.** Raise the riot baton straight across the body until the baton is parallel to the ground (see figure 3-9, page 3-8).
- **Step 2.** Bring the riot baton straight down in front of the body, bending at the knees and keeping the body upright until the long portion of the riot baton is just below the knees. The riot baton should be horizontal and parallel to the ground as it absorbs the shock from an upward strike.

Chapter 3

The support hand fingers should be open and behind the long portion of the riot baton when blocking the object to protect the fingers from being injured by the strike.
- **Step 3.** Assess the situation following a low block, and take appropriate follow-up action, as needed.

Figure 3-8. High block (steps 1 and 2)

Figure 3-9. Low block (steps 1 and 2)

Strong-Side Block

3-27. A strong-side block is very effective in blocking a horizontal strike directed at the strong side of the head, neck, chest (or flank), or hip area. The horizontal strike may be from an individual's foot, fist, elbow, or knee or from a weapon. To perform a strong-side block, the Soldier performs the following steps:
- **Step 1.** Raise the riot baton straight across the body in a vertical position where the grip portion is in the strong hand and the long portion is in the support hand (see figure 3-10).
- **Step 2.** Turns body laterally by rotating the hips toward the strong side and moving the riot baton across the body, keeping the riot baton vertical (see figure 3-10).
- **Step 3.** Assess the situation following a strong-side block, and take appropriate follow-up action as needed.

Equipment and Techniques

Figure 3-10. Strong-side block (steps 1 and 2)

3-28. The strong-side block provides protection for a Soldier from the front to the rear of the body. A riot baton held in the vertical position absorbs the shock of a strike coming from the strong side. The fingers of the Soldier's support hand should be open and behind the long portion of the riot baton when blocking the object to protect the fingers from being injured by the strike.

Support-Side Block

3-29. A support-side block is very effective in blocking a horizontal strike directed at the support side of the head, neck, chest, or hip area. The horizontal strike may be from an individual's foot, fist, elbow, or knee or from a weapon. To perform a support-side block, the Soldier performs the following steps:
- **Step 1**. Move the riot baton in a vertical position toward the support side, ensuring that the grip portion is pointing straight down and the long portion is pointing straight up.
- **Step 2**. Keep the fingers of the support hand open and behind the long portion of the riot baton when blocking the object to protect the fingers from being injured by the strike. At the moment of contact with the opposing strike, the blocking surface of the long portion should be at a right angle to the opposing object.
- **Step 3**. Assess the situation following a support-side block, and take appropriate follow-up action as needed.

Middle Block

3-30. A middle block is very effective in blocking a front horizontal strike directed at the face, throat, chest, abdomen, or hip. The horizontal strike may be from an individual trying to tackle near the waist or shove or punch at the face. To perform a middle block, the Soldier performs the following steps:
- **Step 1**. Move the riot baton toward the middle of the body at a 45° angle, keeping the long portion pointed up and slightly forward of the grip portion (see figure 3-11, page 3-10).
- **Step 2**. Keep the fingers of the support hand open and behind the long portion of the riot baton when blocking the object to protect the fingers from being injured by the strike. However, the support hand may have to grip the long portion when pushing an individual away or forcing an individual down on the ground if the individual is trying to tackle.
- **Step 3**. Assess the situation following a middle block, and take appropriate follow-up action, as needed.

Figure 3-11. Middle block

Riot Baton Striking Techniques

3-31. Seven strikes can be executed using the riot baton. Two of these strikes come from the outside-arm or vertical carry. The other five strikes come from the two-hand carry.

One-Hand Forward Strike

3-32. The one-hand forward strike is a very quick and effective offensive strike. It is usually employed as a countermeasure to an attack from the front that has been blocked effectively.

3-33. Target areas can be as high as the outside upper arm, down to the outer thigh region. An effective one-hand, forward strike must be aggressively quick, with the purpose of distracting, disabling, or altering behavior. Therefore, those employing this technique must be sensitive to what part of the riot baton they use to strike the individual. Strike the target with the last 2 to 4 inches of the long end for optimal results.

3-34. When selecting available targets, consider proper placement according to the zones discussed in figure 3-4, page 3-4. The one-hand, forward strike is employed in one of three ways:
- A horizontal manner.
- A downward diagonal manner to destabilize an individual.
- A vertical manner in front of the body to clear an aggressor's hands.

Note. When the one-hand, forward strike is used in a vertical manner, keep the long portion straight up, not angled forward. By keeping the long portion up rather than angled forward, the chance of striking the individual in the face or head is significantly reduced. For the counterstrike to be effective, follow through with the technique when the baton makes contact with the aggressor or the object to destabilize them. A pattern of movement such as a forward shuffle, forward pivot, strong-side step, or rear pivot may enhance this technique.

Equipment and Techniques

> **WARNING**
>
> This technique is used with the expandable riot baton in the nonextended position. Do not execute the one-hand, forward strike with the 36-inch wooden baton or expandable riot baton in the extended position. It has been shown to cause injury to the wrist.

3-35. When using the vertical or outside-arm carry position, the Soldier quickly moves the riot baton across the body using the strength and power of the hips, swinging the baton from the strong side through the support side (see figure 3-12). Ending this strike leaves the riot baton positioned under the support-side armpit in preparation for the one-hand, reverse strike (see figure 3-12). When delivering this strong-side strike technique (in a horizontal or downward diagonal manner), ensure that the palm is facing up. In a vertical delivery, the palm will be toward the chest rather than up. Pause following the one-hand, forward strike and assess the situation. Take appropriate follow-up action, as needed. If the situation does not call for additional strikes, do not strike again.

Outside-arm carry | **Forward strike** | **Target assessment**

Figure 3-12. Forward strike

One-Hand, Reverse Strike

3-36. The starting position for the one-hand, reverse strike is under the support-side armpit (see figure 3-13, page 3-12). The one-hand, reverse strike is used as a follow-up strike and is quick and effective.

3-37. Target areas can be as high as the outside upper arm, down to the outer thigh region. An effective one-hand, reverse strike must be aggressively quick, with the purpose of distracting, disabling, or altering behavior. Therefore, those employing this technique must be sensitive to which part of the riot baton they use to strike the individual. Strike the target with the last 2 to 4 inches of the riot baton for optimal results.

3-38. When selecting a target, consider proper placement according to the zones discussed in figure 3-4, page 3-4. A Soldier may employ a one-hand, reverse strike in one of the following ways:
- A horizontal manner.
- A downward diagonal manner to destabilize an individual.
- A vertical manner (in front of the body to clear an aggressor's hands).

Chapter 3

Figure 3-13. Reverse strike

3-39. When the one-hand, reverse strike is used in a vertical manner, keep the long portion straight up, not angled forward. By keeping the long portion up rather than angled forward, the chance of striking the individual in the face or head is significantly reduced.

3-40. The one-hand, reverse strike is considered a follow-up strike to the one-hand, forward strike. As a follow-up strike, it is important that Soldiers are taught the discipline of assessing the target. An aggressor may not require another strike, based on the condition and actions after enduring the one-hand, forward strike.

3-41. When using the one-hand, reverse strike, the Soldier quickly moves the straight baton across the body, using the strength and power of the hips (from support-side to strong-side). When the strike is completed, the Soldier's arm will be back in the outside-arm carry position. The Soldier ensures that the palm is facing down when delivering the counterstrike in a horizontal or diagonal manner. This will prevent injury to the user's wrist. In a vertical delivery, the palm will be toward the chest rather than up. Following the one-hand, reverse strike, assess the situation and take appropriate follow-up action, as needed. If the situation does not call for additional strikes, the Soldier should avoid striking again.

3-42. When the one-hand, reverse strike is used in a vertical manner, keep the long portion straight up, not angled forward. By keeping the long portion up rather than angled forward, the chance of striking an individual in the face or head is significantly reduced. For the counterstrike to be effective, follow through with the technique when the baton makes contact with the aggressor or the object to destabilize them. A pattern of movement such as the forward shuffle, forward pivot, strong-side step, or rear pivot may enhance this technique.

WARNING

This technique is used with the expandable riot baton in the nonextended position. Do not execute the one-hand, reverse strike with a 36-inch wooden baton or expandable riot baton in the extended position. It has been shown to cause injury to the wrist.

Two-Hand, Strong-Side, Horizontal Strike

3-43. The two-hand, strong-side, horizontal strike starts from the two-hand carry position and is aggressively quick. The purpose of this strike is to create distance, distract, disable, or alter behavior. Strong-side, horizontal strikes are quick and effective offensive strikes, usually employed as a countermeasure to close frontal attacks that have been effectively blocked.

3-44. The two-hand carry position enables Soldiers to use riot batons at the 24 or 36 inch length. To effectively employ this strike, use the strength and power of the hips to thrust the riot baton in a horizontal manner. Simultaneously, pull back with the support hand as the strong hand drives the grip end toward the target, striking a rib or the abdominal region of the aggressor (see figure 3-14). A pattern of movement, such as a forward shuffle or forward pivot, can enhance this technique. Following the two-hand, strong-side, horizontal strike, assess the target before following up with another strike. An aggressor may not require another strike, based on his condition and actions after an initial strike.

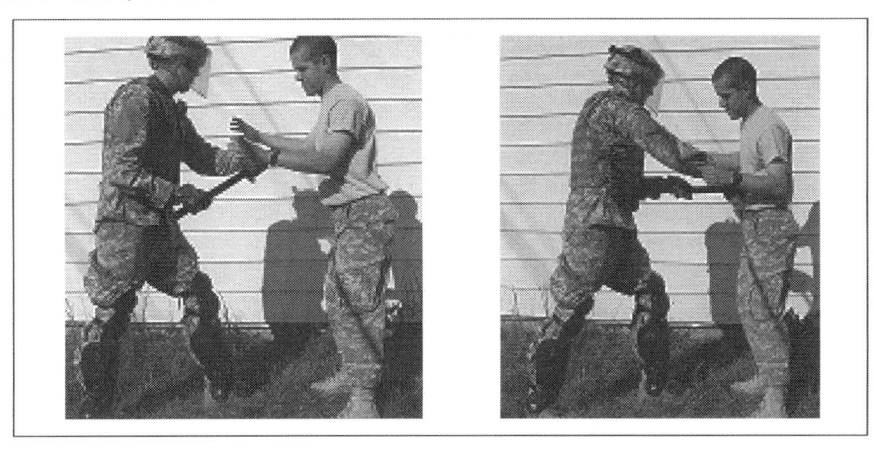

Figure 3-14. Two-hand, strong-side, horizontal strike

Two-Hand, Support-Side, Horizontal Strike

3-45. An effective two-hand, support-side, horizontal strike must be aggressively quick to create distance, distract, disable, or alter behavior. The support-side, horizontal strike is a quick and effective offensive strike usually employed as a follow-up strike to the strong-side, horizontal strike. It is a countermeasure designed for close frontal attacks that have been effectively blocked. Maintaining a strong defensive stance after employing a strong-side, horizontal strike puts the Soldier in position to execute a two-hand, support-side, horizontal strike.

3-46. Use of the two-hand carry position enables Soldiers to use riot batons at 24 or 36 inches. To effectively employ this strike, use the strength and power of the hips to thrust the riot baton in a horizontal manner. Simultaneously, pull back with the strong hand as the support hand drives the grip forward toward the aggressor, striking a rib or the abdominal region of the target (see figure 3-15). A pattern of movement, such as a forward shuffle or forward pivot, can enhance this technique. Following the two-hand, support-side, horizontal strike, it is important to assess the aggressor. An aggressor may not require another strike, based on his condition and actions after an initial strike.

Figure 3-15. Two-hand, support-side, horizontal strike

Chapter 3

Two-Hand, Front Jab

3-47. The two-hand, front jab starts from the two-hand carry position. It is aggressively quick and creates distance, distracts, disables, or alters behavior. Front jabs are effective offensive strikes, usually employed as a countermeasure to charging and overpowering frontal attacks.

3-48. Use the strength and power of the hips to effectively employ this strike in a slightly downward or horizontal manner. Simultaneously, use both arms to shoot the long end of the riot baton straight out from the body to the target area. Immediately, pull back the riot baton to the two-hand carry position.

3-49. Forward jabs drive the long end of the riot baton toward the aggressor, striking a rib, a hip flexor, or the abdominal region (see figure 3-16). A pattern of movement, such as a forward shuffle, enhances the power of this technique. Following the two-hand, front jab, it is important that Soldiers assess the aggressor before following through with another strike, as the aggressor may not require another strike.

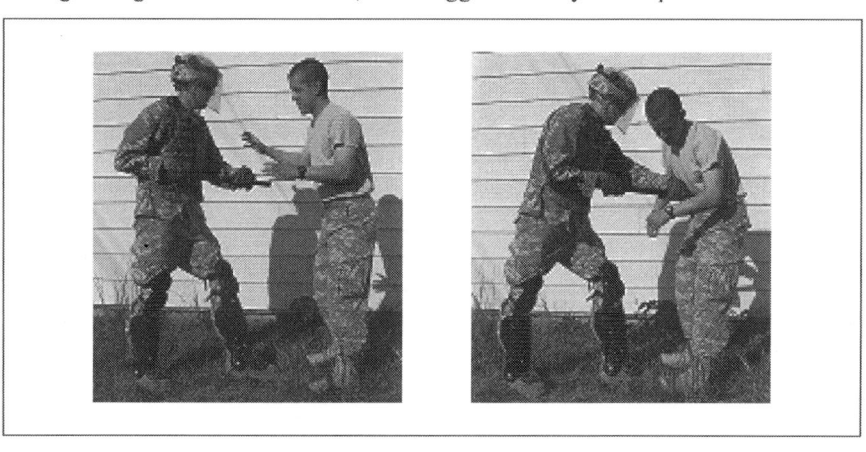

Figure 3-16. Front jab

Two-Hand, Rear Jab

3-50. Starting from the two-hand carry position, the two-hand, rear jab is aggressively quick and creates distance, distracts, disables, or alters behavior. Rear jabs are quick and effective offensive strikes usually employed as a countermeasure to charging and overpowering attacks from the rear.

3-51. To effectively employ this strike, a Soldier turns the head to the rear to identify the target. Then the Soldier uses the strength and power of the hips to thrust the riot baton slightly downward or in a horizontal manner (see figure 3-17). They use both arms to shoot the riot baton back from the body to the targeted area and immediately pull back the riot baton to the two-hand carry position. A pattern of movement, such as a rear shuffle, enhances the power of this technique.

Figure 3-17. Rear jab

Two-Hand, Middle Strike

3-52. The two-hand, middle strike starts from the two-hand carry position. It is aggressively quick and creates distance, distracts, disables, or alters behavior. It is proven to be an effective follow-up technique to a two-hand support- or strong-side block or to destabilize an individual by pushing him back and away. The two-hand, middle strike is used as a two-count movement.

3-53. To perform a two-hand, middle strike (see figure 3-18) the Soldier does the following:
- **Step 1**. Brings the riot baton up to chest level and slightly off parallel to the ground.
- **Step 2**. Steps forward aggressively, simultaneously thrusting the long portion of the riot baton forward in a horizontal manner. Both arms are fully extended at the end of the movement with a quick snappy return to the Step 1 position. Use the entire body to generate the power.

Figure 3-18. Two-hand, middle strike

Riot Baton Retention

3-54. A common technique an aggressor may use is grabbing for a Soldier's riot baton or, in some cases, even taking the riot baton and using it against the Soldier. This causes a disruption or distraction.

3-55. Maintaining physical control of the riot baton is essential for the safety of the Soldier and the control force as a whole. Aggressors will generally attempt to grab the riot baton where they can get the strongest hold. Soldiers must resist the instinct of getting into a tug-of-war match over the riot baton, which often proves to be ineffective.

3-56. Using the momentum of the aggressor to pull the riot baton away, the Soldier simply steps into or closer to the aggressor with the support-side foot. With the momentum created, the aggressor's hold on the riot baton is lessened. The Soldier then rapidly uses the tracing-C technique to retain control of the riot baton.

3-57. The movement of the tracing-C technique's wraps the aggressor's arms around themselves, and then causes them to release the baton. A Soldier using the tracing-C technique does the following:
- **Step 1**. Pushes up on the riot baton.
- **Step 2**. Pulls the riot baton down and around in an upward swing as if tracing a C in the air from bottom to top with the long end.
- **Step 3**. Drives (immediately with a quick and forceful movement) the long end of the riot baton straight down, as if slicing the C in half (see figure 3-19, page 3-16).

3-58. Once the Soldier reaches the top of the C and the aggressor is tied up, it is impossible for the aggressor to maintain hold of the riot baton. Further actions such as a strike may or may not be necessary. Soldiers must be able to assess the situation and react accordingly.

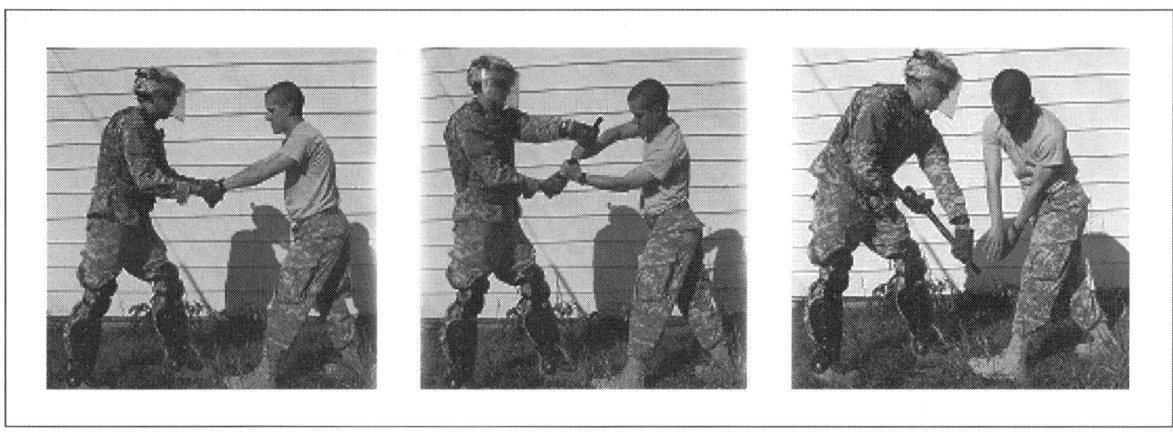

Figure 3-19. Tracing-C technique

ADDITIONAL PROTECTIVE EQUIPMENT

3-59. Along with the riot batons and riot shields, there are additional pieces of equipment (face shields, elbow pads, shin guards, protective vests, and ballistic riot shields) that increase the effectiveness of a control force. These items provide the individual Soldier with added protection to the sensitive and vital areas of the body. They also provide excellent protection for the Soldier from trauma often inflicted from thrown objects (rocks, bricks, sticks, bottles).

RIOT FACE SHIELDS

3-60. All Soldiers operating in a civil disturbance environment should be outfitted with riot face shields. The riot face shields have two adjustable positions and are designed to fit securely on the Soldier's helmet. A nonballistic riot face shield is constructed of hard, durable plastic and protects the Soldier's head, face, and neck from thrown objects (see figure 3-20). It is also designed to be worn over the Soldier's chemical protective mask if needed. Nonballistic face shields are not bullet-resistant.

3-61. Units can also obtain ballistic riot face shields for use in civil disturbance missions. The ballistic face shield is constructed of acrylic and bullet-resistant materials that provide the wearer with Level IIIA protection. Because of the extra weight, ballistic riot face shields should not be worn for standard riot control formations. They are best suited for use within specialized teams associated with the riot control mission; for example, teams responsible for the search and apprehension of identified criminals or for building or alley clearing.

Figure 3-20. Nonballistic riot face shield

SHIN GUARDS

3-62. All Soldiers operating in a civil disturbance environment should be outfitted with shin guards. They are designed to protect the Soldier's feet, shins, and knees from thrown objects or strikes. The nonballistic shin guards are constructed from durable plastic and are easily fastened to a Soldier's legs. They are not bullet-resistant.

3-63. Units can obtain ballistic shin guards for use in civil disturbance missions. Ballistic shin guards are constructed of bullet-resistant materials (Kevlar®), and provide the Soldier with Level IIIA protection to the feet, shins, and knees. They also protect the Soldier from hand-thrown objects. Because of the excessive weight (7 to 10 pounds), ballistic shin guards should not be used as part of the standard riot control formation. Instead, they are best suited for use within specialized teams that are responsible for the search and apprehension of identified criminals or for building or alley clearing. (See figure 3-21 for shin guards.)

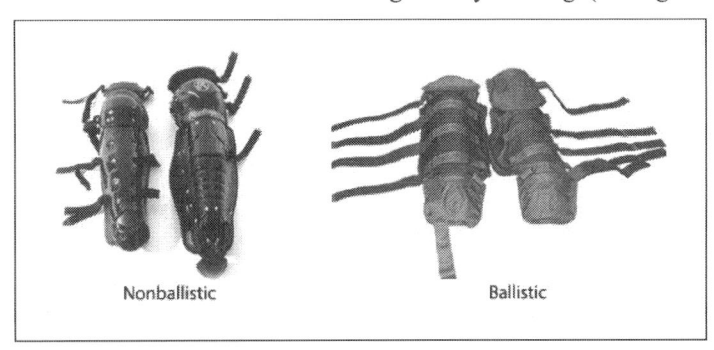

Figure 3-21. Shin guards

BALLISTIC RIOT SHIELDS

3-64. Units may obtain ballistic riot shields for civil disturbance missions. They are constructed from bullet-resistant material that provides Level IIIA protection to the face, torso, and upper legs. Because of its excessive weight (18 or more pounds), the ballistic riot shield should not be used as part of a standard crowd control formation. They are best suited for use within specialized teams for search and apprehension of identified criminals, or for building and alley clearing. (See figure 3-22 for a ballistic riot shield.)

Figure 3-22. Ballistic riot shield

FIRE EXTINGUISHERS

3-65. During civil disturbance response missions, especially with the control force, having fire extinguishers available is highly recommended. As stated earlier, individuals in a crowd may use incendiary devices such as Molotov cocktails against the control force. With a Soldier behind the front line of shields carrying a fire extinguisher, the control force has the ability to quickly respond to, and put out, a fire near or on other control force members before there is a chance of serious injury or the shield line.

TEAM WORK

3-66. Teamwork is essential during civil disturbances. Soldiers should never have to rely solely on their own skills or abilities in riot control missions. Although individual skills are discussed in this chapter, it is important to know that well-trained Soldiers who employ offensive, defensive, riot shield, riot baton, and NLW techniques working as a team will perform the collective task of crowd control well.

TEAM TECHNIQUE FOR RETAINING A RIOT SHIELD

3-67. Riot control operations are dynamic and often chaotic. Soldiers armed with riot shields provide a first line of defense, while those armed with riot batons and firearms provide overwatch as the formation moves toward engaging a hostile crowd. To work effectively and in concert, Soldiers must be properly trained, drilled, and exercised. If an aggressor approaching a line of skirmishers (members of an employed control force) violently grabs a riot shield, help is required to maintain control. A Soldier armed with a 36-inch wooden riot baton or an expandable riot baton (extended to 36 inches) can be of assistance. The Soldier simply moves forward into a gap between the riot shields where he can quickly strike the top or side of the riot shield, slicing the long end across or straight down onto the hands and fingers of the aggressor.

3-68. Riot batons are not the only way to effectively knock an aggressor's hands from a riot shield. Soldiers armed with shotguns or rifles can just as effectively strike the hands or fingers of a persistent aggressor with the barrel of the weapons using the technique described above.

TAP-DOWN TECHNIQUE FOR EMPLOYING NONLELTHAL ROUNDS

3-69. Commanders must be familiar with the characteristics and capabilities of all nonlethal rounds to use them effectively. When shotguns or grenade launchers are used within a line of skirmishers (usually located behind the riot shields), it is imperative that a method is developed, trained, and practiced to effectively operate as a team. Operators of these weapons may encounter problems in riot control situations when trying to identify and effectively engage legitimate targets. The tap-down technique is used to enhance target identification and engagement with nonlethal munitions. If ordered to engage targets or the situation authorizes an engagement, Soldiers armed with nonlethal munitions may step forward, level the weapons, and fire upon legitimate targets.

3-70. A Soldier who is armed with a NLW and is using the tap-down technique must first tap on the shield holder's shoulder. Tapping on the shield holder's shoulder alerts them that the gunner is preparing to fire. In response to the tap, the shield holder drops to one knee while keeping the riot shield firmly affixed to the front for protection. The gunner takes a step forward and fills the gap. The gunner then leans into the riot shield bearer's back with the knee and fires. This technique ensures that the long end of the weapon is extended beyond the riot shield.

3-71. Once Soldiers firing munitions have fired, they raise the weapon back to a high-port arms. The Soldiers clear the weapons and tap the riot shield bearer a second time, signaling them to rise to a standing position.

PUSH/PULL WITH VERBAL COMMANDS TECHNIQUE FOR EMPLOYING NONLETHAL ROUNDS

3-72. Another technique for employing nonlethal rounds from a line of skirmishers on a legitimate target is the push/pull with verbal commands technique. This technique is basically an evolution of the tap-down technique discussed above, and is seen by many as a superior method.

3-73. A Soldier who is armed with a NLW and is using the push/pull with verbal commands technique will step forward and physically grab the shield holder's shoulder area, give a command such as, "Nonlethal, get down" and then physically push the shield holder down. The shield holder goes down to one knee while keeping the riot shield firmly affixed to the front for protection. The nonlethal gunner leans into the shield bearer's back with their knee and fires, ensuring that the end of the weapon is extended beyond the shield.

3-74. After firing, the nonlethal gunner raises the weapon back to a high-port arms and clears the weapon. The nonlethal gunner then physically grabs the shield bearer's shoulder area and gives a command such as,

"Nonlethal clear, get up." The nonlethal gunner then helps pull the shield holder back up, and the shield holder resumes the position with the line.

3-75. This technique is considered superior to the tap-down technique since it employs more physical contact and verbal commands so that the shield holder knows exactly what is happening. If the shield holder is expecting the tap-down method there may be confusion at times when, during a skirmish line, something accidentally taps a shield holder and they get down, and this was not the intent.

WARNING

The long end (barrel) of the weapon must be projected beyond the riot shield before firing. This is a critical safety step, which prevents nonlethal projectiles from hitting the riot shield or Soldier and causing injury.

WEAPON POSITIONS

3-76. The primary method of carrying weapons in the control force formation is at the safe-port position (see figure 3-23). It allows the Soldier to control both ends of the weapon while moving in and out of the formation and advancing on the crowd.

3-77. High-port position (see figure 3-23) is a position of complete readiness. It is used whenever troops are in contact with a crowd that is showing resistance or not withdrawing. This is a tiring position and is hard to maintain for extended periods. Commanders must rest the troops at every opportunity by using less tiring positions.

Figure 3-23. Weapon positions

This page intentionally left blank.

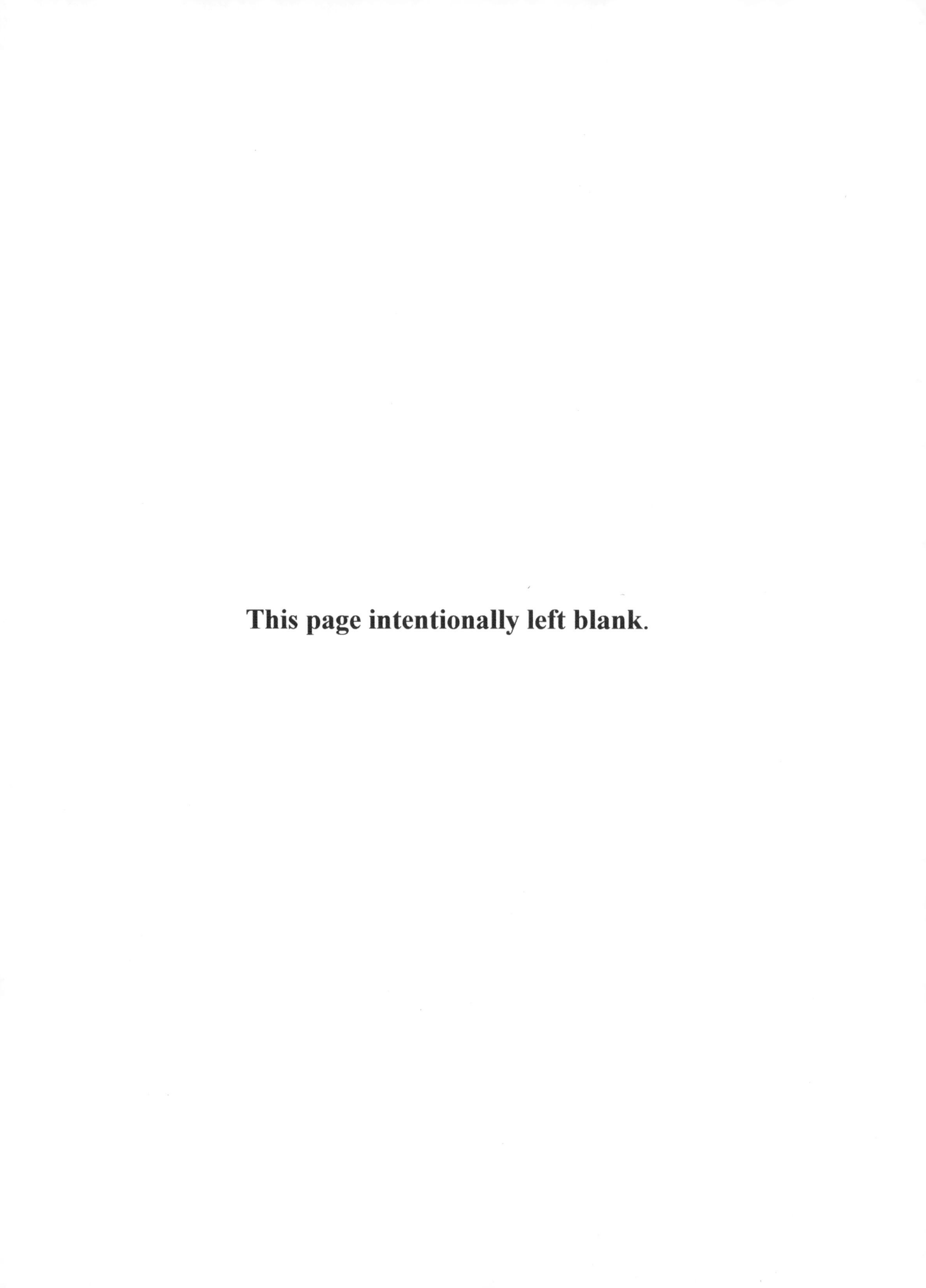

Chapter 4
Control Force Formations

In any civil disturbance situation, the commander of the responding unit has many options for controlling the crowd. These options include holding discussions with crowd leaders, making proclamations over loudspeakers, displaying a show of force, and employing NLW from a distance based on level of threat and the use of force continuum. The use of proper risk management helps the commander determine the course of action. If the determination is made that the crowd must be dispersed or moved and is unwilling to do so on its own, the control force is employed. A control force has multiple tactics and techniques that can be utilized in varying situations. Control force formations, when properly employed and executed against a crowd, are some of the most effective methods of crowd control.

GENERAL INFORMATION

4-1. Control force formations are used to disperse, contain, or block a crowd. These formations are more effective in urban areas. When the control force is employed in urban areas, it is easier to split a crowd into smaller segments, isolate instigators, or funnel the crowd into the desired location by using buildings and other man-made structures. Commanders must be mindful of the fact that well-organized crowds may attempt to move to the flanks of a formation or get behind the formation to gain a positional advantage.

Note. Figure 4-1 is a symbol key for the formation figures in this chapter and appendix B.

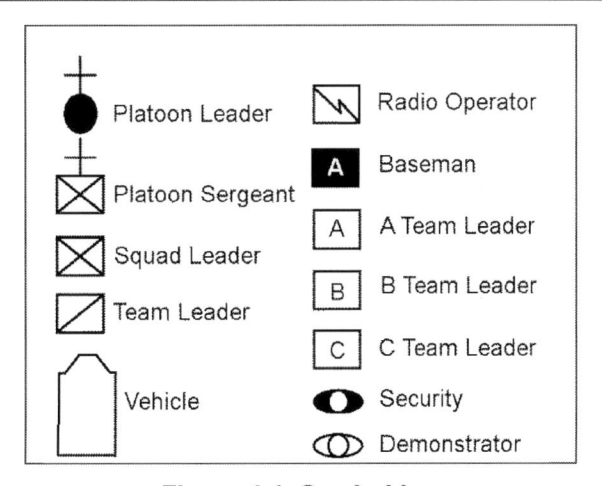

Figure 4-1. Symbol key

4-2. With the use of NLW, it is possible to create an effective standoff distance (15 to 100 meters) between the crowd and the control force. It is also possible to advance on and disperse the crowd without coming into direct contact with it.

4-3. Commanders must be aware of the limitations of control force formations. They are not the answer to all civil disturbance situations. Do not expose the formation to sniper fire or unnecessary violence simply for a show of force. Control force formations should be used when it is decided that a crowd poses a threat and must be dispersed or moved to a specified area. If considering dividing a large crowd, the commander must consider that this might not solve the problem. It may worsen the problem by creating smaller elements that may engage the control force in small-mob tactics, such as sniping, looting, burning, and attempting to envelop the control force. These tactics can be defeated by area control measures, such as building searches, patrolling, and other tactics. After dispersing the crowd, the control force must not assume that there will be an immediate return to peaceful activities. The use of formations is only part of the total dispersal effort.

4-4. Commanders must assess and secure the area that the control force will be operating in. This may be accomplished with the use of helicopter overflights and by visually securing rooftops, high elevations, and vantage points. DM/observer teams may be used to secure the rooftops and provide lethal overwatch for the control formation. The control force commander must be aware that DM teams are positioned on rooftops.

4-5. Crowd control formations and the support teams have more capabilities than just crowd dispersal. They also have the capability to apprehend and detain certain members of the crowd that the commander feels may instigate the crowd to further violence, or those individuals who have blatantly committed a crime. Commanders must analyze the threat, determine the mission of the control force, and decide which control force formations will accomplish that mission according to METT-TC.

4-6. During civil disturbance missions the crowd is primarily made up of civilians. However, commanders must analyze and prepare for any potential opposition. The formations discussed in this chapter are guidelines and may be adapted to fit any mission or situation. Whatever the modification, Soldiers must stay in position and on line. Through training and rehearsals, Soldiers become proficient in basic formation movements and are able to adjust to changing situations. Soldiers must also be prepared to move up or down on the levels of force continuum based on the situation.

ACTIONS BEFORE MOVEMENT

4-7. A commander is prudent to include civil disturbance training in the annual training plan of the unit. If the unit deploys to an area where civil disturbances are a recurring event, sustainment training must occur more frequently.

4-8. Before moving the control force to the rally point, an intense rehearsal must be conducted by the leadership and the control force. A top-down review of the ROE and RUF must be accomplished. The ROE and RUF must be part of the unit training plan and each Soldier must be trained to standard. The use of NLW (type-specific) must be granted to the on-site commander from the approval authority.

4-9. Before moving the control force to the civil disturbance area and into a potentially hostile urban environment, the commander and staff must review the preincident plans and expand them (as needed) based on current information. Because of the employment of forces against ambiguous threats, IPB becomes critical. Information is the key to developing an appropriate response to civil disturbances.

4-10. During the planning phase (see chapter 2), the information provided by the IPB will aid the staff in selecting various routes and rally points. The selection of ingress and egress routes must include a variety of ways in and out of the area. Direct and indirect routes and those with cover and concealment are necessary. The rally point must be cleared and secured by an advance party capable of controlling the area.

ACTIONS AT RALLY POINT

4-11. Once at the rally point, the commander makes contact with the local police, civil authorities, or military officer. He then assesses the situation, decides the next course of action, and issues orders, as appropriate. The platoon sergeants (PSGs) form the platoons into a column formation and place the team leaders directly in front of the teams (see figure 4-2). Team and squad leaders make last minute checks of the Soldiers and await orders.

4-12. The commander places the lethal overwatch (DM teams) in areas that overlook the control force and the crowd. They may be to the flanks and slightly to the front of the formation. It is the DM team responsibility to protect the formation from lethal fire by constantly scanning the crowd.

4-13. When the commander receives word that DM teams are in place, the control force is put into a crowd control formation and is moved quickly from the rally point to where the crowd is assembled. Depending on the situation, movement should be in a column formation or one of the three basic control force formations (line, echelon, and wedge). Reserve forces are left at the rally point until ordered forward as additional lethal overwatch or to reinforce the formation.

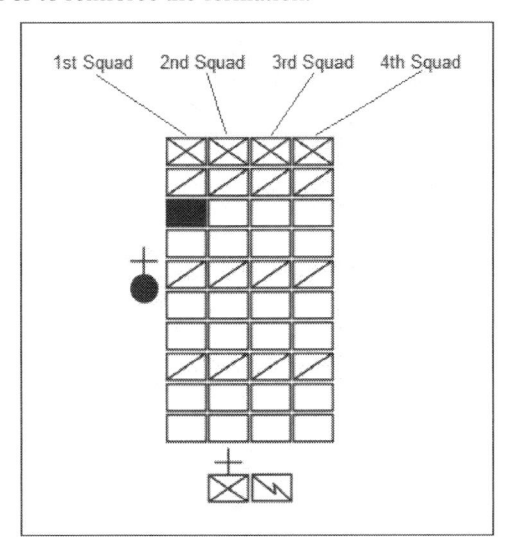

Figure 4-2. Column formation

FORMATIONS

4-14. Control force formations, when properly employed and executed against a crowd of limited size, are one of the most practical methods of crowd control. Experience has indicated that the most frequently used control force formations are the line, echelon, and wedge. The two lesser-used formations are the diamond and circle. Descriptions of all the formations are as follows:

- **Line formation**. The line formation is the basic formation, and it is used more often because of its offensive and defensive applications. As an offensive formation, the line formation is used to push or drive crowds straight back, across an open area, or up a city street. As a defensive formation, the line formation is used to hold the crowd or to deny access to areas.
- **Echelon formation**. The echelon formation is an offensive formation, and it is used to turn or divert groups in open or built-up areas and to move crowds away from buildings, fences, and walls.
- **Wedge formation**. The wedge formation is an offensive formation that is used to penetrate and split crowds into smaller groups.
- **Diamond formation**. The diamond formation, when used as an offensive formation, is used to enter a crowd. It is the formation of choice for extraction teams. As a defensive formation, the diamond formation is used when all-around security is required in open areas. The decision to use this formation is based on the conformation of the crowd.
- **Circle formation**. The circle formation is used for the same purpose as the diamond formation. The decision to use this formation is based on the conformation of the crowd.

4-15. There are many suitable variations of the control force formations that may be employed, but appropriate commands and signals must be created to execute the formations. Because of the somewhat complicated nature and the coordination required for these formations, new variations must be trained, practiced, and rehearsed before they are used in a civil disturbance.

4-16. Training must also enforce Soldier understanding of the need to stay formed for individual protection. Individual Soldiers are much more vulnerable to attack when they break ranks and chase after crowd members. When an individual Soldier breaks ranks, they not only put themselves in danger, but they also put the entire formation in danger.

Vehicles and Formations

4-17. Military vehicles may be employed with the control force formation when determined by METT-TC. They present a strong psychological effect and offer protection for the occupants. Wheeled armored vehicles are best because they do not deface the pavement. Whenever vehicles are used in a crowd control formation, the commander must ensure that he is still able to see and control the formation. This may require him to occupy a position in a similar vehicle behind the formation or command subordinate leaders to move away from the front line and into the line of sight control. This will require additional hand-and-arm signals to allow the commander and subordinate leaders to communicate. Commanders can effectively use vehicles as primary communication tools by using horns and lights as signals to organize movement or actions. However vehicles are used, it takes a good measure of training and practice for them to be effective.

4-18. Although vehicles add strength to formations, certain precautions must be taken. Covering the windshield with sturdy, close-mesh fencing and the standard safety glass will offer some level of protection to the occupants. Shields or mobile barriers may be built by using barbwire to mount wooden or metal frame strung with across the front of a vehicle. Members of the formation should walk as near to the front corners of each vehicle as possible to keep rioters from attacking the sides and rear of the vehicles.

Elements of a Control Force Formation

4-19. There are four elements that make up the basic crowd control formation. They are as follows:
- **Base element**. The base element is made up of two ranks. The first rank is shield holders, while the second rank contains the NLW. This is the front line of the formation.
- **Support element**. The support element forms up in a column formation behind the base element and has a variety of uses. It may be used to replace base element members as needed, provide lateral or direct support, or perform extraction team operations. The support element helps the base element by performing the following essential tasks:
  - *General support.* The general-support element is formed from an uncommitted squad in the platoon. When a company is tasked as the control force element, one of the platoons becomes the general-support element. The element is in a column formation centered on and behind the main formation. From this formation, the general-support element can move to lateral or direct support, as needed.
  - *Lateral support.* The lateral-support element is used to protect the flanks of the formation. This is done by moving a set number of teams forward from the general-support element or by using the end teams in the formation; however, this will make the formation smaller. Once in position, these teams become part of the formation, with a riot shields facing the flanks of the formation.
  - *Direct support.* When direct support is ordered, the general-support element moves forward as they move into a formation. While moving forward, the squad and team leaders from the control force formation step back and allow the riot shield holders from the support element to step behind riot shield holders of the original formation. This allows the support riot shield holders to form up between and behind the riot shield holders of the original formation. Now, there are two lines of riot shield holders between the crowd and NLW firers. This formation is the strongest of the formations and requires more planning and practice to master.
- **Command element**. The command element contains several different members. A general configuration for the command element is the platoon leader, the PSG, a radio operator, a video recorder operator (if used), and an interpreter (if required). This element does not have a fixed location within the formation and moves about as needed.
- **Lethal overwatch element**. The lethal overwatch element is a team formed from reserve security forces.

4-20. The reserve support element is not part of the control force formation until it is brought forward from the rally point to join the formation. It remains until released by the formation commander. Lethal overwatch teams are formed from the reserve force. Once lethal overwatch teams are deployed and in position, they are under the control of the formation commander. Communication between the lethal overwatch team and the formation commander is a priority because the commander approves target selection and engagement.

COMMANDS

4-21. Verbal commands are given to the control force formation. Verbal commands for the on-guard position are given in one count. All other commands are given in two counts, a preparatory command followed by a command of execution. However, verbal commands cannot be relied on completely, so commanders must plan to use hand-and-arm signals (see figure 4-3).

Line
Raise both arms from the sides until they are horizontal. The arms and hands should be extended with the palms down.

Echelon (Right or Left)
Extend one arm 45° above the horizontal and the other 45° below the horizontal. The arms and hands should be extended. The upper arm shows the direction of the echelon when the commander faces the troops.

Wedge
Extend both arms downward and to the sides at a 45° angle. The arms and hands should be extended with the palms down and in.

Diamond
Extend both arms above the head. Bend the elbows slightly, and touch the fingertips together.

Circle
Give the diamond signal, then give a circular motion with the right hand.

Figure 4-3. Hand-and-arm signals

4-22. Verbal commands are the primary method for communication during control force missions. When vehicles are part of the formation, radios become an alternate method for relaying commands. To improve communication, commanders may use hand-and-arm signals with verbal commands. The basic commands used in control force formations are outlined in table 4-1, page 4-6. These commands can be added to or combined to form more complex commands, therefore forming more complex formations.

Table 4-1. Control force basic commands

Commands	Command	Given By	Purpose
Formations	Platoon on line	Platoon leader or commander	To form a line formation
	Platoon wedge	Platoon leader or commander	To form a wedge formation
	Platoon echelon	Platoon leader or commander	To form an echelon formation
	Platoon diamond	Platoon leader or commander	To form a diamond formation
	Platoon circle	Platoon leader or commander	To form a circular formation
	Move	Platoon leader or commander	As a command of execution. **Note:** The platoon leader or commander also identifies the location for the formation by pointing the arm to the desired location for the formation.
Support	General support	Platoon leader or commander	To place a specified unit in the rear of the base element
	Lateral support	Platoon leader or commander	To place support elements on the left or right flank of the base element
	Direct support	Platoon leader or commander	To move support elements forward to strengthen the base element
	Open	Extraction team leader	To open a space in the formation
	Up	Extraction team leader	To inform the extraction team to start moving back to the main formation
Fire	Weapon system gunners, number of rounds, type of rounds, and prepare to fire	Platoon leader or commander	To ready nonlethal gunners to fire weapons; for example, grenade launcher gunners, three rounds, area target, prepare to fire
	Shield down	nonlethal gunners	To tell riot shield holders to get down on one knee and lower the riot shield to the ground.
	Shield up	nonlethal gunners	To tell riot shield holders to stand and raise the riot shield
Weapons	Port arms	Platoon leader or commander	To use when not in contact with the crowd
	High port	Platoon leader or commander	To tell nonlethal gunners what position to hold the weapons in while the formation is in physical contact with the crowd. This allows for rapid targeting and firing of nonlethal munitions

MOVEMENTS

4-23. Control force formations move in the same manner as regular formations. This allows the commander to maneuver the formation by commanding the number of steps it should move and in what direction, such as "Five steps, forward march." The normal rate of march for entering and leaving a control force formation is double-timing. The half-step march is used when the formation is in direct contact with the crowd. This slows the formation down and allows for better mission command. The squad and team leaders echo preparatory commands and provide cadence while in control force formations.

Control Force Formations

INTERVAL AND DISTANCE

4-24. Interval is the lateral space between elements. Distance is the space between elements in a column. The usual interval and distance between Soldiers in control force formations is 30 inches. The interval and distance can be adjusted based on METT-TC. If the crowd has to be physically pushed back, a close interval is preferred. This allows the riot shields to be overlapped, creating a stronger wall. During peaceful demonstrations, the interval could increase to double arm width, allowing the formation to cover more area and still control the crowd. The interval and distance could change several times during the course of operations before the crowd is dispersed.

EXTRACTION TEAMS

4-25. The extraction team is a squad (see figure 4-4) that is generally formed from the support element, but could also be formed from reserve security forces (if this squad has four teams, the formation commander may incorporate the fourth team into the formation or use them as a reserve for the squad). Once the team is formed, the formation commander has operations control until the team mission is complete and it returns to the rear of the formation. This team provides the riot control formation with the means to employ NL and lethal cover forward of the formation. During control force missions, extraction teams conduct the following:

- Extract vehicles or personnel that are in immediate danger from the crowd.
- Detain and escort downed rioters to the rear of the formation.
- Detain and search subjects (done by the identified apprehension team).
- Cover confined or congested areas where a full riot control formation cannot be inserted.

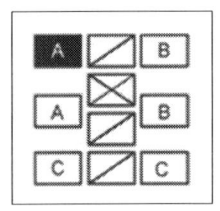

Figure 4-4. Extraction team formation

4-26. The extraction team is usually a squad; however, based on METT-TC, it can be smaller or larger. While the recommended distance for deploying the extraction team from the control force formation is no farther than 10 meters, this too may change based on METT-TC. The control force formation protects the extraction team and provides immediate support, if necessary.

4-27. The extraction team may deploy from anywhere within the formation. When given orders to deploy, the squad leader of the extraction team gives the formation commands, identifies at least two personnel in the squad to be the apprehension team that conducts the search and apprehension of the subject. The squad leader leads the squad to the base line of the formation. He then extends his arm between the two riot shield holders and commands, "Open," while tapping the riot shield holders on the side of the shoulder. The two riot shield holders take one step backward and one step to the right or left. This clears a path for the extraction team. The extraction team leader then states the number of personnel leaving the formation, such as "Ten security personnel leaving." As the last extraction team member exits the formation he states, "Last man." The two riot shield holders then return to the original position in the formation. The adjacent base element squad or team leaders pass the number of personnel in the team through the formation.

4-28. As the extraction team approaches an instigator or incapacitated demonstrator, the riot shield holders envelop the target and face in the direction of the nearest threat. Nonlethal gunners on the left and right cover the respective areas. The search and apprehension team immediately controls and restrains the target. To avoid confusion, one team member concentrates on controlling the subject while another team member applies a restraining system. When the search and apprehension team has the subject under control, the extraction squad leader sounds off with, "Up." Upon hearing the "Up" command, it is repeated by all extraction team members. Team members then grab a shoulder of the team member in front of them to backtrack into the formation. As the extraction team approaches the formation, the nearest base element leader will extend his arm and command, "Open," while tapping the riot shield holders on the side of the shoulder. The riot shield holders move one step backward and to the right or left to open the formation. As he enters the formation, the extraction team leader sounds off with the number of personnel entering the formation, such as "Ten security personnel and one demonstrator." The adjacent base element leader counts the number of personnel as they enter the formation. When the last man enters the formation, he states, "Last man." The riot shield holders then return to the original places in the formation. The adjacent squad and team leaders in the base element pass the information through the formation that the extraction team has returned.

LETHAL OVERWATCH TEAMS

4-29. During a nonlethal engagement, the use of a DM team provides confidence and safety to those facing the mob. If a lethal threat is presented, the DM team in an overwatch position (armed with a standard military rifle that is mounted with a high-powered scope) can scan the crowd, identify agitators and riot leaders for apprehension, or fire lethal fire if so ordered or warranted. It is also ideally suited for flank and counter-sniper operations.

4-30. The DM team sets the security overwatch and provides real-time intelligence and reporting that is vital to mission success. It provides coverage during the entire approach to the crowd, and its ability to select positions and provide cover fire (if and when warranted) is critical to the safety of the control force. Successful execution requires training, practice, and rehearsal with the control force formation.

4-31. The DM team is organized from a standard three- or four-Soldier team. Each individual on the team is equipped with a standard-issue weapon. One individual has a rifle with a scope, another has a set of binoculars, and two other individuals provide security for the team. Each team is equipped with a radio for communication with the headquarters element of the control force formation.

4-32. The teams must have a visual advantage over the crowd to provide lethal protection to the formation. This is best accomplished by placing them on nearby rooftops, in the upper floors of buildings, and on hilltops. They must have the optical equipment to identify mob leaders, instigators, and individuals with weapons. Team integrity must be maintained. With three-Soldier teams, the positions are marksman, observer, and security. If a team has four Soldiers, the fourth can be utilized as additional security, or another option is outfitting them with a camera to record events.

4-33. Two teams should be deployed to cover the flanks of the formation. Each team should be deployed to a position that is in front of the formation and in an overwatch position. The number of teams deployed is based on METT-TC. As the formation moves forward, the teams leapfrog forward from the formation.

4-34. The reserve forces, located at the rally point, can provide another lethal force of some size that can be brought forward, as needed. Each Soldier in the control force formation should have a sidearm or a rifle. The rifle is slung diagonally across the back with the rifle butt over the left shoulder and the muzzle below the right hip. Lethal munitions are in a separate ammunition pouch that is isolated from nonlethal munitions. This is to prevent the mixing of nonlethal and lethal ammunition.

RESERVE FORCES

4-35. A large reserve of Soldiers should be maintained during civil disturbance operations. Knowing that a large reserve force is available provides confidence and safety within the control force and helps prevent them from overreacting to provocative acts with disorderly and criminal elements in the crowd. When determining the number of reserve forces required, it should be resolved in favor of a large number. Lethal overwatch teams, forces to augment the control force, and apprehension teams come from the reserve forces.

4-36. Apprehension teams are a must when it is likely that a large number of people will be apprehended. These teams provide an organized response to what could be a chaotic situation. The teams can be organized at the team or squad level, depending on the number of apprehensions expected. These teams usually operate behind the base element. During peaceful demonstrations, these teams can be sent forward to remove demonstrators who refuse to disperse.

SQUAD FORMATIONS

4-37. The smallest formation is a squad formation, which is used in back of the main formation (usually a company formation) to cover side streets. Squad members must know the positions regardless of which control force formation they are in, squad to company.

> *Note.* Three-team squads have been used in the following squad formation diagrams. When squads have four teams (for example, a Military Police Squad), the fourth team can be added to the formation or used as a reserve team for the squad formation.

4-38. When moving a squad into a crowd control formation from a column formation, the squad leader takes one or more steps to the right of the squad and faces it. The squad leader gives the command and hand-and-arm signal for the formation they want. Then they indicate where the formation is to be located by pointing in that general direction. The A team leader commands, "Follow me," and places the baseman at the position indicated by the squad leader. The squad forms on the baseman position.

LINE FORMATION

4-39. The command for forming a squad in a line formation is, "Squad line formation, move." On the command of execution, the A team leader leads the baseman to the place indicated by the squad leader. The squad members align themselves in sequence with the baseman at normal intervals (see figure 4-5). Based on the situation, the squad leader may designate a specific interval. They do this when giving the preparatory command. If no interval is specified, the squad automatically forms using the normal interval.

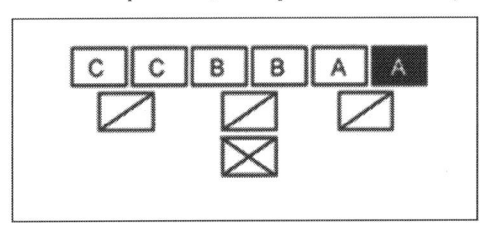

Figure 4-5. Squad line formation

ECHELON FORMATION

4-40. The command for having a squad form in an echelon formation is, "Squad echelon right (or left), move." On the command of execution, the A team leader places the baseman at the location indicated by the squad leader. The squad members align themselves in sequence with the baseman; one pace to the side and one pace to the rear (see figure 4-6).

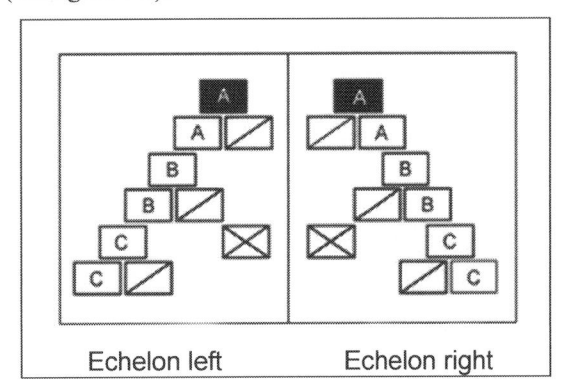

Figure 4-6. Squad echelon formations

Wedge Formation

4-41. The command for moving a squad formation into a wedge formation is, "Squad wedge, move." On the command of execution, the A team leader moves the baseman to the place indicated by the squad leader. The A team lines up to the left of the baseman, one pace to the left and one pace to the rear of each preceding man. B team members align themselves with the baseman, one pace to the right and one pace to the rear of each preceding man. C team members align themselves in the same way to the left of the baseman (see figure 4-7).

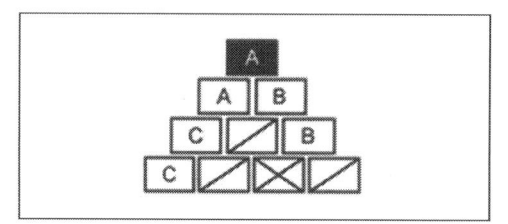

Figure 4-7. Squad wedge formation

Assembly

4-42. When assembling a squad from the line formation, the squad leader takes a position at a sufficient distance to the rear of the squad and commands, "Squad assemble." At the same time, the squad leader raises the right hand in the air and makes a circular motion. The A team leader and the baseman do an about-face movement.

4-43. The other squad members face toward the baseman. On the command of execution, "Move," the squad leader points to the place where he wants the squad to assemble. The A team leader double-times to the designated spot, and the other members of the squad follow. Team leaders fall into the file in the designated positions as they move to the assembly area (AA). To assemble from a squad echelon formation, the steps are the same as a line formation.

4-44. To assemble from a squad wedge formation, the squad leader takes the same steps as for the line and echelon formations. The B team members do a half left face, and the A team and C team members do a half right face. The C team pauses at the baseman position and allows the B team to clear the formation before moving to the AA.

Diamond and Circle Formations

4-45. The diamond and circle formations are used during extraction team operations. They are small formations used to penetrate the crowd or cover small areas. The decision on which formation to use is based on METT-TC and the ability of the squad to perform.

4-46. Commands for forming a squad in a diamond or circle formation is, "Squad diamond (or circle), move." On the command of execution, the A team leader moves the baseman to the place indicated by the squad leader. The A team lines up to the left of the baseman, covering the 9 to 12 o'clock positions. B team members align themselves to the right of the baseman, covering the 1 to 5 o'clock positions. C team members align themselves covering the 6 to 8 o'clock positions (see figure 4-8).

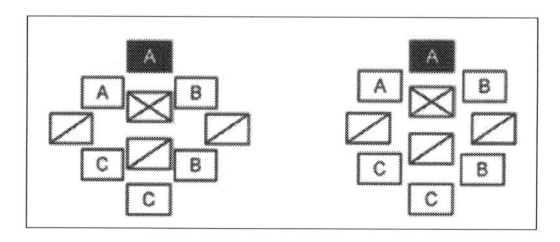

Figure 4-8. Squad diamond or circle formation

4-47. To assemble from a squad diamond or circle formation, the squad leader takes the same steps as he would for a line formation. The A team leads the squad to the AA followed by the B team and then the C team. Teams fall into a column formation as they file back to the AA.

PLATOON FORMATIONS WITH THREE SQUADS

4-48. The platoon headquarters consists of the following individuals: the platoon leader, the PSG, and a messenger or radio operator. When directed by the platoon leader, other individuals such as the selected marksman, interpreter, RCA disperser operators, and firefighters may augment the platoon headquarters. In forming all control force formations from the column, the platoon leader moves to the right of the platoon and faces them when giving commands. Along with the preparatory command, the platoon leader gives the hand-and-arm signal. On the command of execution, "Move," the platoon leader points to the approximate location where they want the platoon to form. The platoon leader pauses between the preparatory command and the command of execution to allow each squad leader to issue a preparatory command to the squad.

PLATOON LINE FORMATION

4-49. The command for forming a platoon line is, "Platoon on line, move." Immediately following the platoon leader's preparatory command, the squad leaders of the 1st and 3d squads give the command, "Follow me." The leader of the 2d squad gives the command, "Stand fast." On the platoon leader's command of execution, the 1st and 3d squads move forward to the point designated by the platoon leader. The 1st team member of the 1st squad is the baseman for the platoon formation. The 1st squad forms a squad line to the left of the baseman while the 3d squad forms a squad line to the right of the baseman and dresses with the 1st squad. After the 1st and 3d squads have cleared the platoon, the 2d squad leader gives the command, "Follow me." The 2d squad splits and the A and B teams form a line to the right of the 3d squad. The C team (with the squad leader) forms a line to the left of the 1st squad (see figure 4-9).

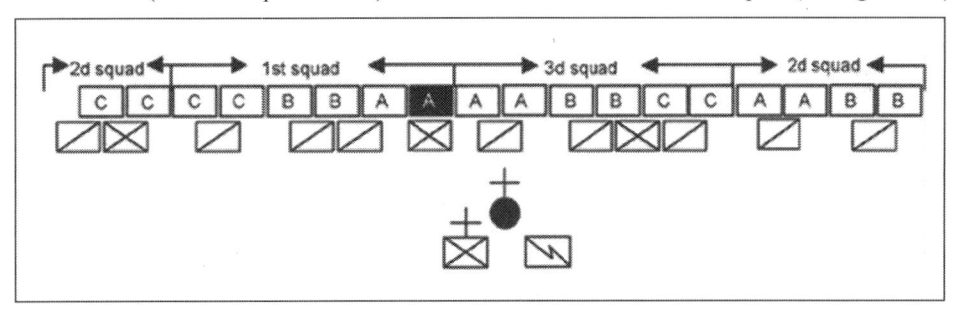

Figure 4-9. Platoon line formation (three squads)

Assembling From a Platoon Line Formation

4-50. When assembling the platoon from the platoon line formation, the platoon leader and the headquarters personnel take a position to the rear of the platoon. The platoon leader then gives the command, "Platoon assemble," while raising the right arm and making a circular motion above the head. Platoon members automatically assume the port arms position. The 1st squad leader and the baseman do an about face. The 3d squad leader moves to the head of the squad. All other members do an about-face movement toward the baseman. On the platoon leader's command of execution, the platoon leader points to where they want the platoon to assemble. The 1st squad leader gives the command, "Follow me," and moves the squad toward the AA. The squad moves to make a single file line to the baseman position followed by the C team of the 2d squad. As the 1st squad clears the baseman position, the 2d squad leader comes to a halt at the baseman position. The 3d squad leader gives the command, "Follow me," and leads the squad to the AA followed by the A and B teams of the 2d squad. The A team leader of the 2d squad comes to a halt at the baseman position. Once the 3d squad has cleared the baseman position, the 2d squad leader gives the command, "Follow me," and leads the squad to the AA. The 2d squad reassembles into the original column formation as they move to the AA. As the 1st squad comes to a halt (facing the crowd) in the AA, the 3d squad dresses with the 1st squad and leaves space for the 2d squad to return to its place in

Chapter 4

the formation. Once the platoon is formed into a column formation, headquarters personnel take the position in the formation. The PSG, giving commands, moves the platoon to the rally point.

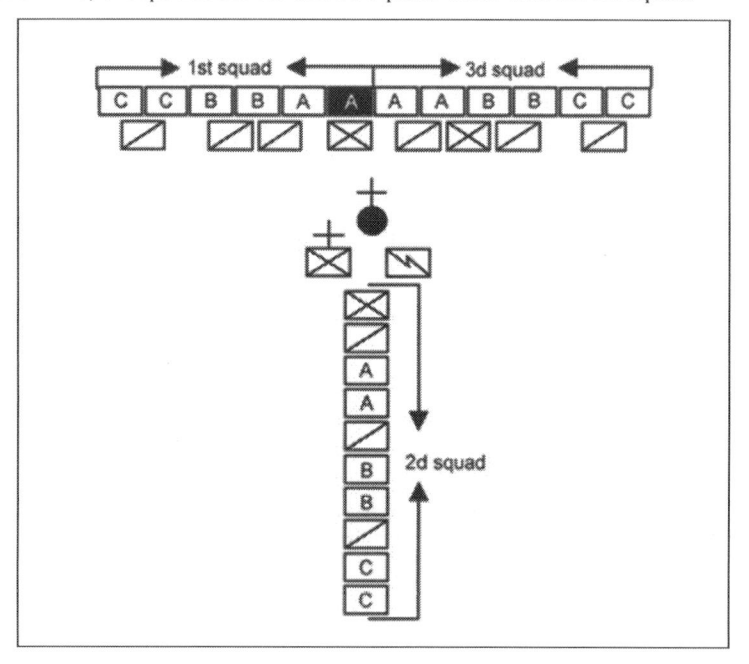

Platoon Line Formation With General Support

4-51. Whenever the command for establishing a crowd control formation contains the phrase "In support" (without modification), it means that the support element is to remain in general support.

4-52. The command for forming a platoon line with the 2d squad in general support is, "Platoon line, 2d squad in support, move." The 1st and 3d squads of the platoon form the line while the 2d squad remains in the column (see figure 4-10). To assemble a platoon with a squad in general support, the procedure is the same as the platoon line, except that the 1st and 3d squads dress with the 2d squad.

Figure 4-10. Platoon line formation with general support

Platoon Line Formation With Lateral Support

4-53. The command for forming a platoon line with 2d squad in lateral support is "Platoon line, 2d squad in lateral support, move." The 1st and 3d squads execute the line as before, and the 2d squad stands fast. After the line has been formed, the 2d squad leader gives the command, "Follow me." The A and B teams move to the right flank while the squad leader and the C team move to the left flank of the formation. The 2d squad forms columns behind the last Soldiers of the line formation. If no direction is given, the 2d squad splits to cover both flanks. A squad may be used to cover one flank by giving the command, "2d squad right (or left) lateral support" (see figure 4-11).

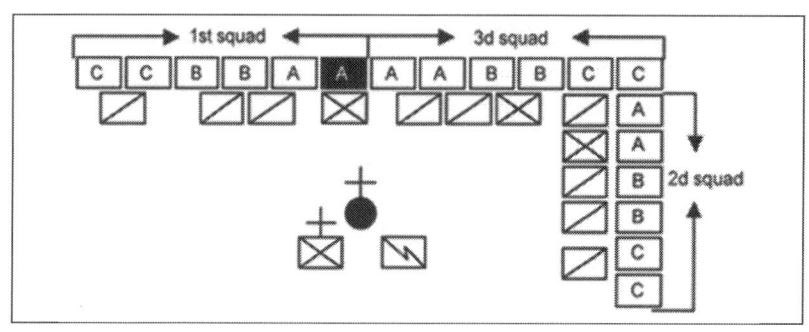

Figure 4-11. Platoon line formation with lateral support (right)

Control Force Formations

4-54. The 2d squad may be moved from general to lateral support at anytime by the platoon leader. The platoon leader commands, "2d squad, lateral support, move." To have the 2d squad join the line from either support position, the platoon leader commands, "2d squad, extend the line, move." The 2d squad leader commands, "Follow me." On the command of execution, the squads set up individual lines, closing and dressing on the existing line. To assemble the platoon from a platoon line formation with lateral support, follow the same steps as for the platoon line.

Platoon Line Formation With Direct Support

4-55. The command for forming a platoon line formation with 2d squad in direct support is "Platoon line, 2d squad in direct support, move." The 1st and 3d squads execute a line as before. The 2d squad executes a squad line directly to the rear and centered on the 1st line. The Soldiers in the supporting line cover the intervals between the Soldiers in the 1st line. To do this, the squad and team leaders of the 1st and 3d squads must take two steps to the rear to allow space for the 2d squad to move into place. After seeing the squad and team leaders move back from the line, the 2d squad leader commands, "Follow me" and leads the squad into position (see figure 4-12).

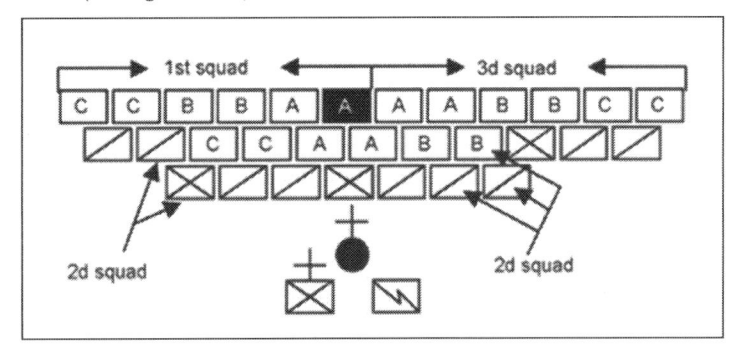

Figure 4-12. Platoon line formation with direct support

4-56. To assemble a platoon formation with direct support, the procedure is the same as the platoon line formation, except that the 2d squad moves to the AA first. To assemble the support squads from any position to general support, the platoon leader commands, "2d squad in support, move." The 2d squad then returns to a column behind the line formed by the other two squads.

PLATOON ECHELON RIGHT AND LEFT FORMATIONS

4-57. The command for forming a platoon echelon right formation is "Platoon, echelon right, move." After the platoon leader's preparatory command, the squad leader of the 1st squad commands, "Follow me." The squad leaders of the 2d and 3d squads command, "Stand fast." On the command of execution, the 1st squad moves out and executes an echelon right at the location designated by the platoon leader. As the 1st squad clears the column, the 3d and 2d squads extend the echelon. The 2d squad performs support to this formation in the same ways it supports a line formation.

4-58. The command for forming a platoon echelon left is "Platoon echelon left, move." The platoon echelon left is formed in the same manner as the echelon right (see figure 4-13, page 4-14). Figure 4-14, page 4-14; figure 4-15, page 4-15; and figure 4-16, page 4-15 show support formations in a left echelon.

4-59. To assemble the platoon, the platoon leader takes up position to the rear of the formation with the platoon headquarters. On the preparatory command, "Platoon Assemble," the 1st squad leader does an about-face movement while all other members assume the port arms position and face the baseman. On the command, "Move," the 1st squad moves first, followed by the 3d and 2d squads. Each squad dresses with the 1st squad as it reaches the AA. The assembly of the echelon right formation is the same as the echelon left.

Chapter 4

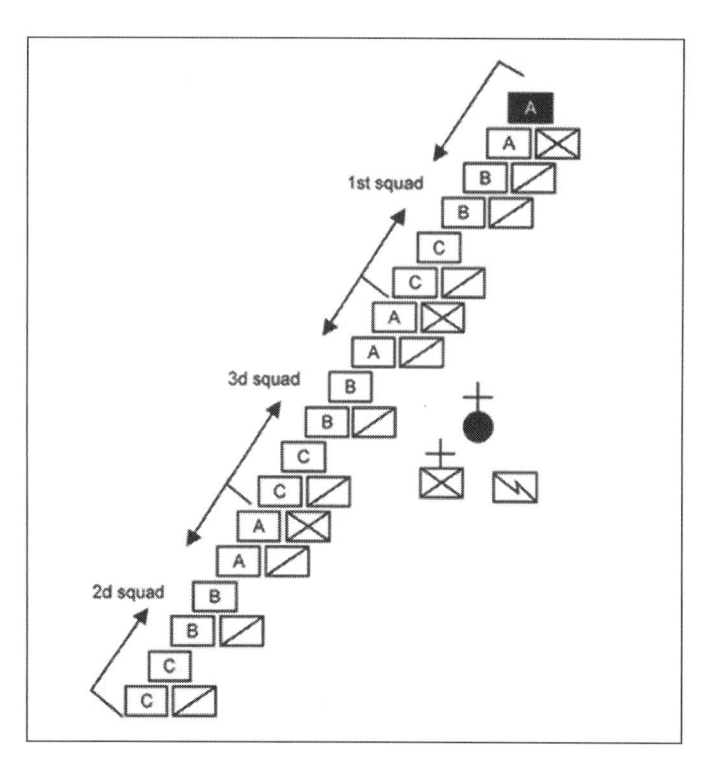

Figure 4-13. Platoon echelon left formation

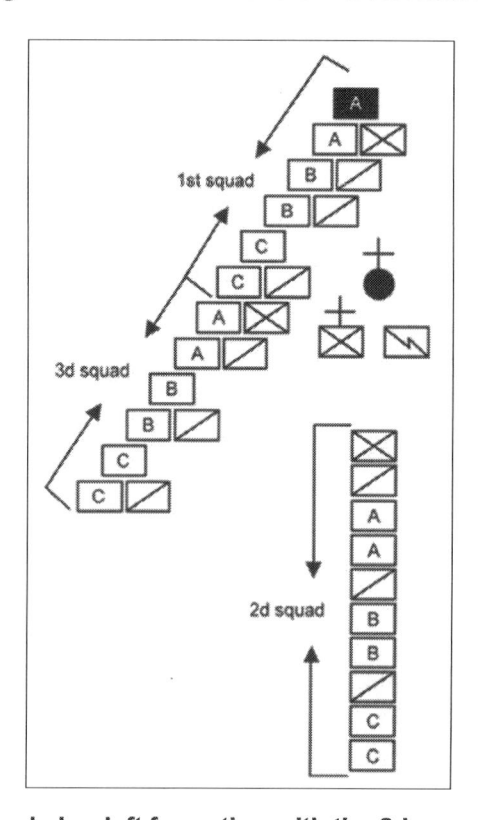

Figure 4-14. Platoon echelon left formation with the 2d squad in general support

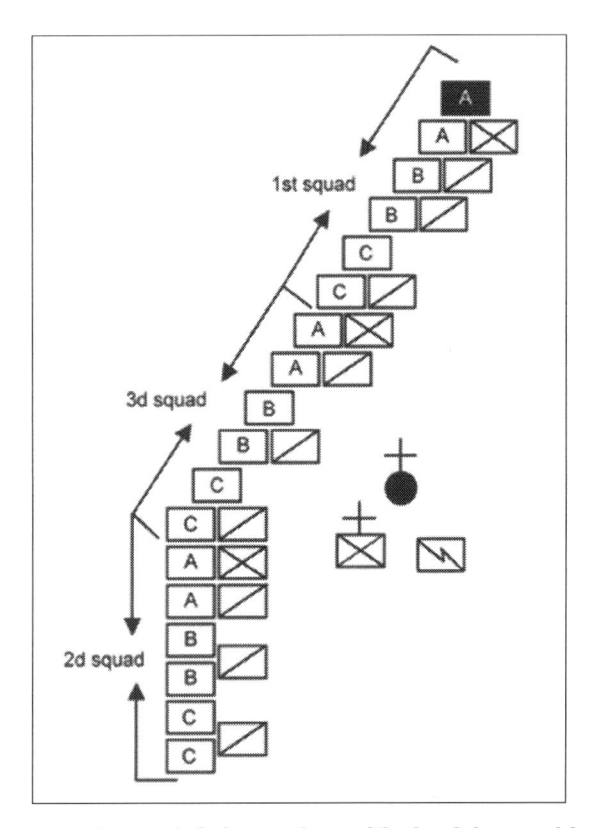

Figure 4-15. Platoon echelon left formation with the 2d squad in lateral support

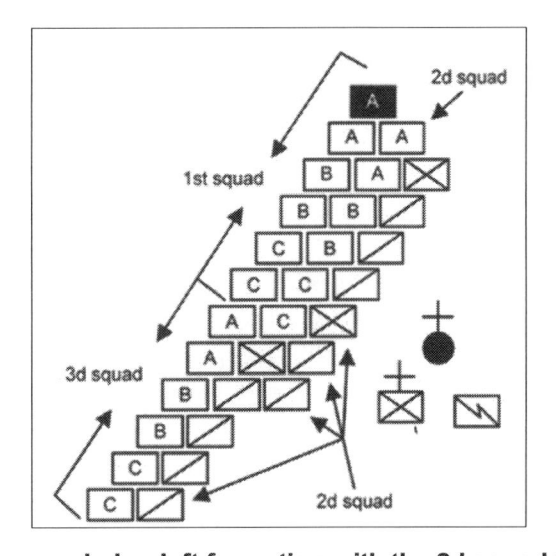

Figure 4-16. Platoon echelon left formation with the 2d squad in direct support

PLATOON WEDGE FORMATION

4-60. The command for forming the platoon wedge formation is "Platoon wedge, move." After the platoon leader's preparatory command, the squad leaders of the 1st and 3d squads command, "Follow me." At the same time, the 2d squad leader commands, "Stand Fast." On the platoon leader's command of execution, the 1st and 3d squads move directly to the front. The 1st squad executes an echelon left on the baseman while the 3d squad executes an echelon right. When the last man of the 1st and 3d squads clear the 2d squad, the 2d squad leader commands, "Follow me," and moves out to the left and right. The 2d squad splits and the A and B teams go to the right and the C team goes to the left to extend the formation (see figure 4-17). Assembly of the wedge formation is the same as the platoon line.

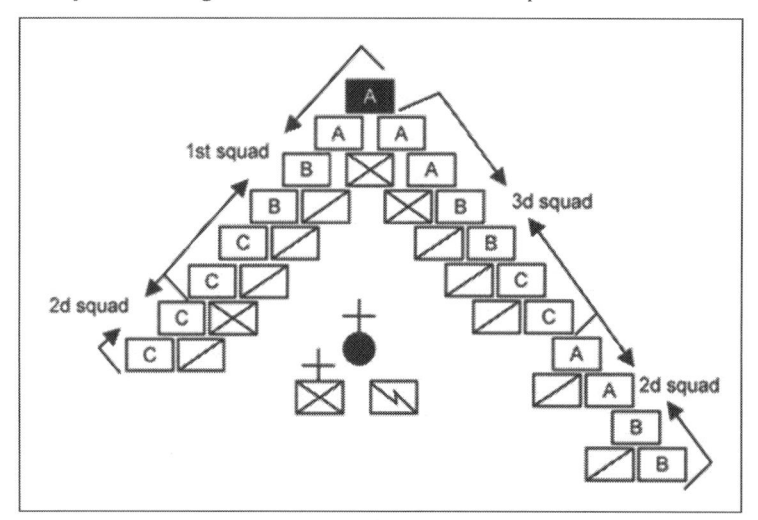

Figure 4-17. Platoon wedge formation

Platoon Wedge Formation With General Support

4-61. The command for forming a platoon wedge formation with support is "Platoon wedge, 2d squad in support, move." The 1st and 3d squads execute the wedge, while the 2d squad remains in a column formation (see figure 4-18).

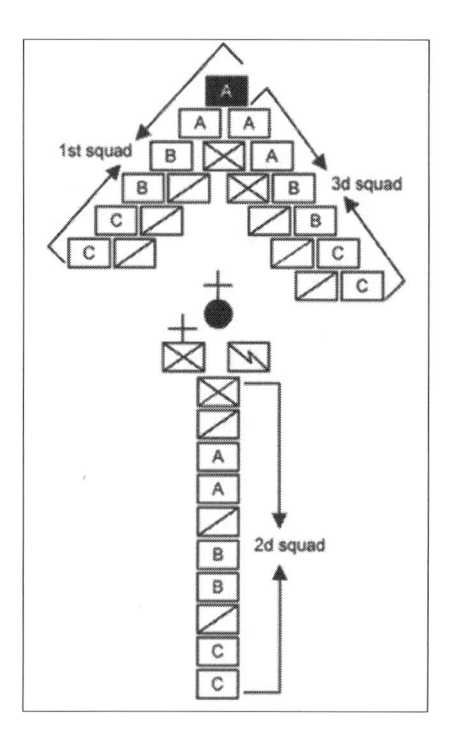

Figure 4-18. Platoon wedge formation with 2d squad in general support

Platoon Wedge With Lateral Support

4-62. The command for forming a platoon wedge formation with lateral support is "Platoon wedge, 2d squad in lateral support, move." The 1st and 3d squads execute the wedge while the 2d squad stands fast.

After the 1st and 3d squads have cleared the column, the 2d squad leader commands, "Follow me." If no direction is given, the 2d squad splits to cover both flanks. A squad may be used to cover one flank by commanding, "2d squad right (or left) lateral support" (see figure 4-19 and figure 4-20).

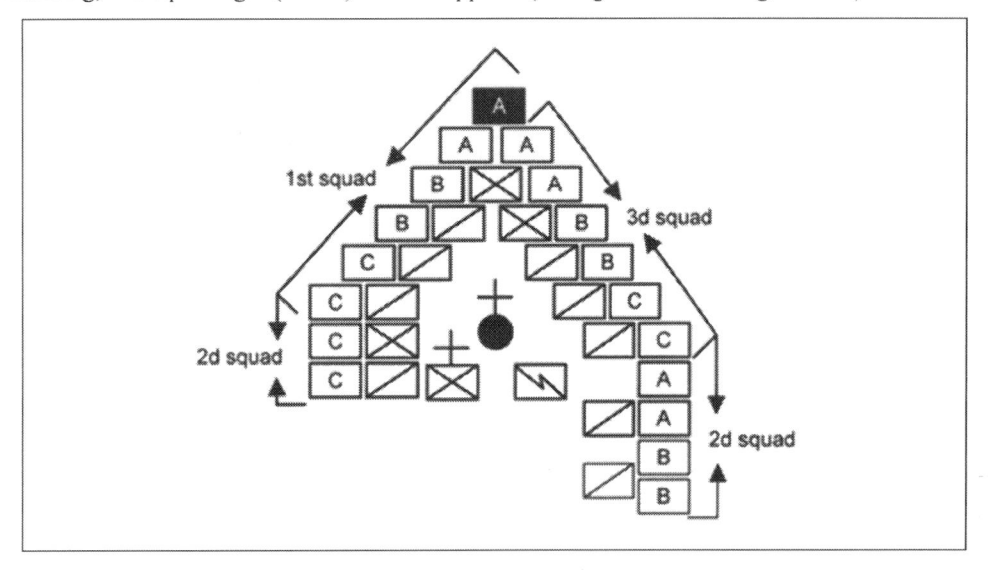

Figure 4-19. Platoon wedge formation with the 2d squad in lateral support

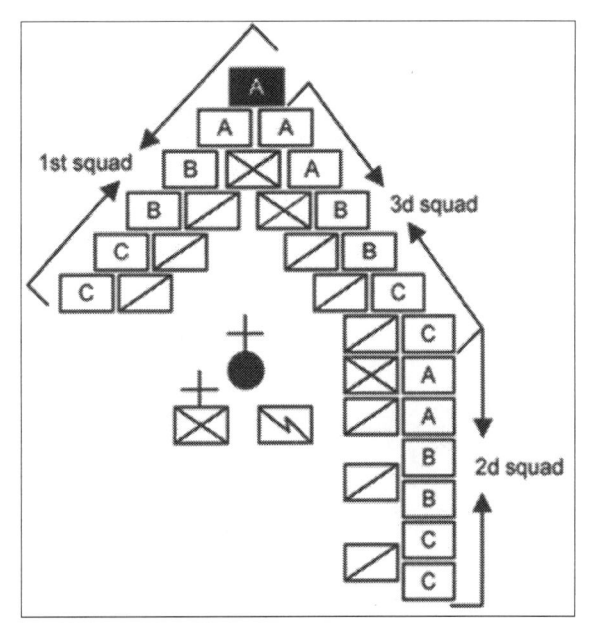

Figure 4-20. Platoon wedge formation with the 2d squad in lateral support (right)

4-63. To move the 2d squad from general support to lateral support, the platoon leader commands, "2d squad, lateral support, move." To have the 2d squad join the wedge from general or lateral support, the platoon leader commands, "2d squad, extend the wedge, move." To extend the wedge, the 2d squad splits and the teams move to the left and right, respectively.

Platoon Wedge With Direct Support

4-64. The command for forming a platoon wedge formation with the 2d squad in direct support is "Platoon wedge, 2d squad in direct support, move." The 1st and 3d squads execute a wedge. The 2d squad waits for the squad and team leaders to move to the rear, as in the line formation, before executing a wedge directly behind and centered on the main formation. The individuals in the supporting wedge cover the intervals between individuals in the leading wedge (see figure 4-21).

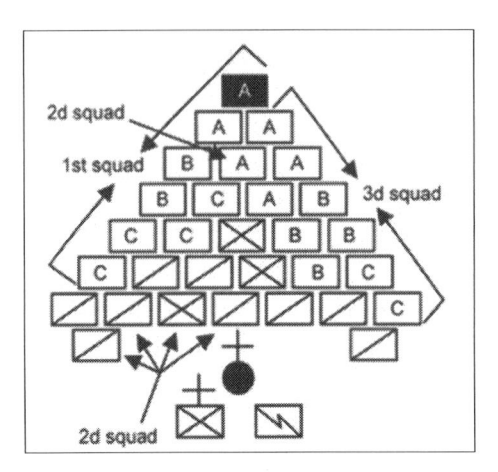

Figure 4-21. Platoon wedge formation with the 2d squad in direct support

PLATOON DIAMOND AND CIRCLE FORMATIONS

4-65. These formations are used in open areas or where the crowd may be able to envelop the formation. The diamond and circle formations are primarily defensive in nature and difficult to maneuver. The decision about which formation to use is based on the ability of the platoon to perform them. The command for having a platoon form in a diamond or circle formation is "Platoon diamond (or circle), move." On the command of execution, the 1st squad leader moves the baseman to the place indicated by the platoon leader. The baseman becomes the 12 o'clock position while the 1st squad lines up to the left of the baseman covering the 8 to 12 o'clock positions. The 3d squad aligns itself to the right of the baseman, covering the 12 to 4 o'clock positions and the 2d squad aligns itself, covering the 4 to 8 o'clock positions (see figure 4-22 and figure 4-23).

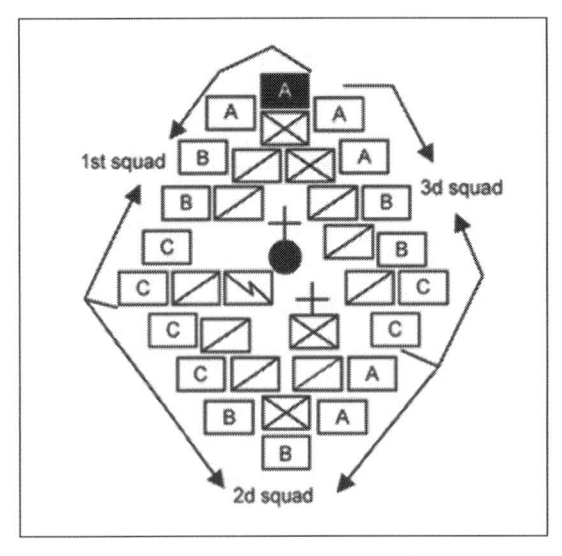

Figure 4-22. Platoon diamond formation

Control Force Formations

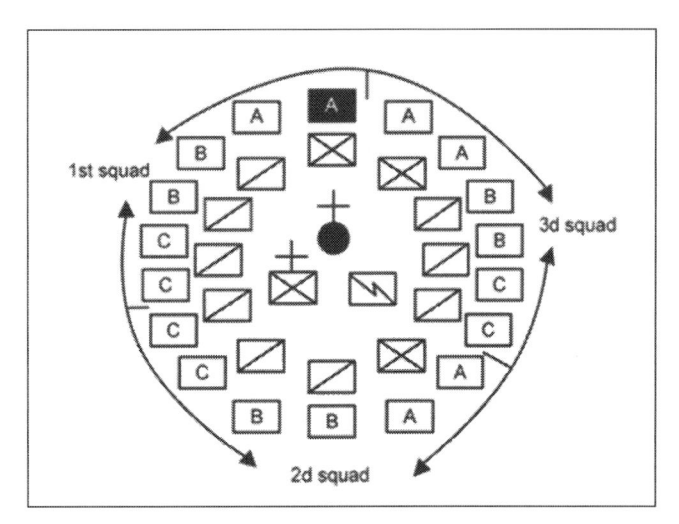

Figure 4-23. Platoon circle formation

4-66. To assemble from a platoon diamond or circle formation, the headquarters element takes the same steps as that of a line formation. The 1st squad leads the platoon back to the AA followed by the 2d and 3d squads. Squads fall into a column formation as they file back to the AA.

RELIEF FOR ELEMENTS IN PLACE

4-67. During crowd control operations, the platoon leader may rotate squads to give them a rest. The platoon leader is not limited to using only those squads specified in the preceding examples as the lead elements of the formations. They can replace the base elements by commanding direct support to the 1st squad and then directing the 1st squad into general support. The support element (the 2d squad) then passes through the 1st squad. Once the 2d squad is formed directly behind the 1st squad, the 1st squad leader commands, "Right face." The members of the 1st squad do a right face movement and the 2d squad steps quickly though the 1st squad and forms the base formation. The 1st squad leader then commands, "Follow Me," and leads his squad to the general support position. This procedure is often necessary when protective masks are used and chemical irritants employed. The 1st squad then replaces the 3d squad in the same manner. Platoons participating in company operations are relieved in the same manner.

PLATOON FORMATIONS WITH FOUR SQUADS

4-68. When forming control force formations from the column, the platoon leader moves to the right of the platoon and faces it when giving commands. The platoon leader gives the hand-and-arm signal and the preparatory command. On the command of execution, "Move," the platoon leader points to the approximate location where he wants the platoon to form. The platoon leader pauses between the preparatory command and the command of execution to allow each squad leader to issue a preparatory command to the squad.

PLATOON LINE FORMATION

4-69. The command for forming a platoon line formation is "Platoon line, move." Immediately following the platoon leader's preparatory command, the squad leaders of the 1st and 4th squads command, "Follow me." The squad leaders of the 2d and 3d squads command, "Stand fast." On the platoon leader's command of execution, the 1st and 4th squads move forward to the point designated by the platoon leader. The 1st A team member of the 1st squad is the baseman for the platoon formation. The 1st squad forms a squad line to the left of the baseman and the 4th squad forms a squad line to the right of the baseman with all lines dressed to the right. After the 1st and 4th squads have cleared the platoon, the 2d and 3d squad leaders command, "Follow me." The 2d squad forms a squad line to the left of the 1st squad. The 3d squad forms a squad line to the right of the 4th squad. All squads dress with the 4th squad (see figure 4-24, page 4-20).

Chapter 4

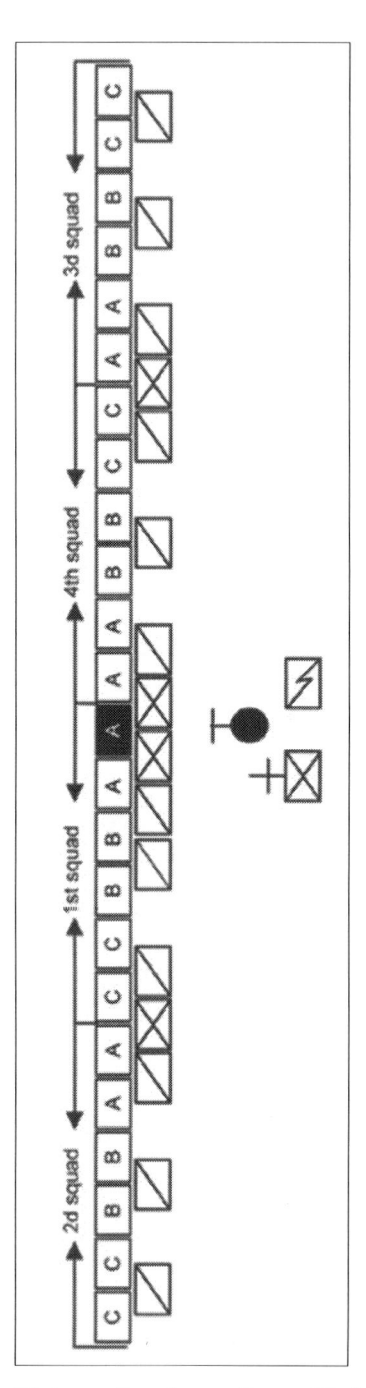

Figure 4-24. Platoon line formation with four squads

Platoon Line Formation Assembly

4-70. When assembling from the platoon line formation, the platoon leader and the headquarters personnel take a position to the rear of the platoon. The platoon leader then gives the command, "Platoon assemble," while raising the right arm and making a circular motion above the head. Platoon members automatically assume the port arms position. The 1st squad leader and the baseman do an about-face movement. All other platoon members do an about-face movement toward the baseman. On the platoon leader's command of execution, the platoon leader points to where they want the platoon to assemble. The squad leader commands, "Follow me," and moves the squad toward the AA. The 1st squad files to the baseman position, followed by the 2d squad. As the 2d squad clears the baseman position, the 4th squad leader then commands, "Follow me," and leads the squad to the AA, followed by the 3d squad. As the 1st squad comes to a halt facing the crowd in the AA, the 2d squad assumes its position to the right of the 1st squad. As the 4th squad assembles, it dresses on the 1st squad, leaving space for the 3d squad to return to its place in the formation. Once the platoon is formed into a column formation, headquarters personnel take a position in the formation. The PSG then commands, "Counter-column, march," and moves the platoon to the rally point.

Platoon Line Formation With General Support

4-71. Whenever the command for establishing a crowd control formation contains the phrase "In support" without any other modification, such as "Lateral," it means that the support element is to remain in general support. The command for forming a platoon line with two squads in general support is "Platoon line, 2d and 3d squads in support, move." The 1st and 4th squads execute the line, while the 2d and 3d squads remain in the column (see figure 4-25). To assemble a platoon with two squads in general support, the procedure is the same as that of the platoon line, except that the 1st and 4th squads dress on the 2d and 3d squads.

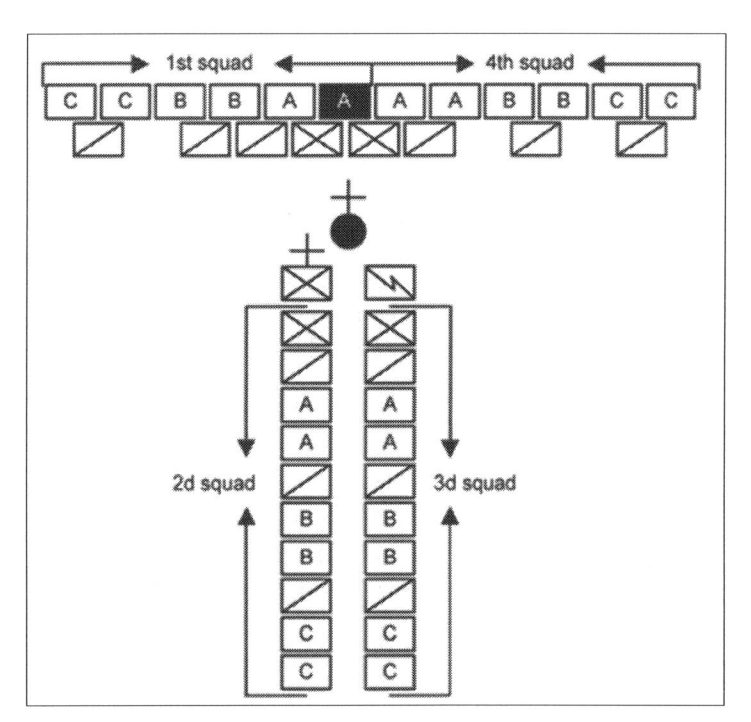

Figure 4-25. Platoon line formation with 2d and 3d squads in general support

Platoon Line Formation With Lateral Support

4-72. The command for forming a platoon line formation with two squads in lateral support is "Platoon line, 2d and 3d squads in lateral support, move." The 4th and 1st squads execute the line as before, and the 2d and 3d squads stand fast. After the line has been formed, the squad leaders of the 2d and 3d squads command, "Follow me." The 2d squad forms a column behind the last man of the 1st squad. The 3d squad forms a column behind the last man of the 4th squad (see figure 4-26, page 4-22).

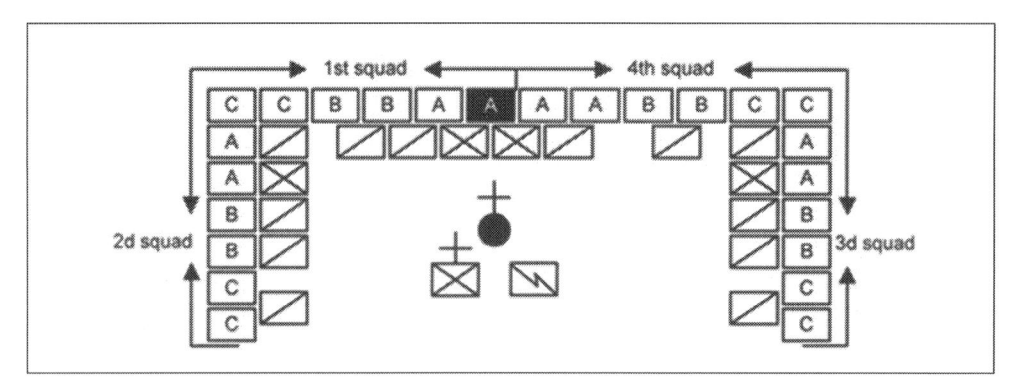

Figure 4-26. Platoon line formation with 2d and 3d squads in lateral support

4-73. Squads may be moved from general support to lateral support at any time by the platoon leader. The platoon leader commands, "2d and 3d squads, lateral support, move." To have the 2d and 3d squads join the line from either support position, the platoon leader commands, "2d and 3d Squads, Extend the line, move." The 2d and 3d squad leaders command, "Follow me." On the command of execution, the squads set up individual lines, closing and dressing with the existing line. To assemble the platoon from a platoon line with lateral support, the procedure is the same as that of the platoon line, except lateral support squads face forward until they move to the AA.

Platoon Line Formation With Direct Support

4-74. The command for forming a platoon line with two squads in direct support is "Platoon line, 2d and 3d squads in direct support, move." The 1st and 4th squads execute a line as before. The 2d and 3d squads execute a second line directly to the rear and centered on the first line. The members in the direct support line cover the intervals between members in the baseline. To do this, the squad and team leaders of the 1st and 4th squads must take two steps to the rear to allow space for the 2d and 3d squads to move into place. After seeing the squad and team leaders move back from the line, 2d and 3d squad leaders command, "Follow me," and lead the squads into position (see figure 4-27).

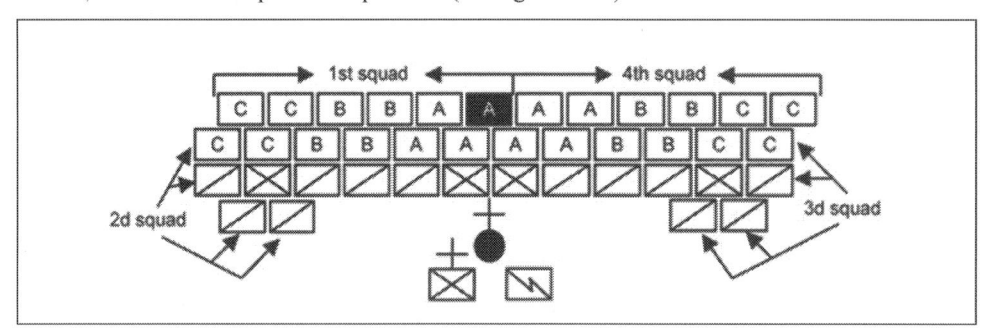

Figure 4-27. Platoon line formation with 2d and 3d squads in direct support

4-75. To assemble the support squads from any position to general support, the platoon leader commands, "2d and 3d squads in support, move." The 2d and 3d squads then return to a column behind the line formed by the 1st and 4th squads. To assemble the entire platoon, the procedure is the same as that of a platoon line, except that the 2d squad moves to the AA first, followed by the 3d, 1st, and 4th squads.

Platoon Line Formation With One Support Squad

4-76. The command for forming a platoon line formation with one squad in support is "Platoon line, 3d squad in support, move." The 1st squad moves out and executes a squad line. The 2d and 4th squads form a line on the side of the left and rights sides of the 1st squad. The 3d squad remains in column formation. The support squad may be used in lateral support on one or both sides of the formation or in direct support of any segment of the formation. To assemble the platoon, the procedure is the same as that of a platoon line, except that all squads dress with the 3d squad.

PLATOON ECHELON RIGHT AND LEFT FORMATIONS

4-77. The command for forming a platoon echelon right formation is "Platoon echelon right, move." After the platoon leader's preparatory command, the squad leader of the 1st squad commands, "Follow me." The squad leaders of the 2d, 3d, and 4th squads command, "Stand fast." On the command of execution, the 1st squad moves out and executes an echelon right at the location designated by the platoon leader. As each squad clears the column, the next successive squad moves out and extends the echelon that has been formed. To assemble the platoon, the procedure is the same as that of a platoon line, except that all squads file back in order.

4-78. The command for forming a platoon echelon left formation is "Platoon echelon left, move." The platoon echelon left is formed in the same manner as the echelon right, but in reverse order (see figure 4-28). To assemble the platoon, the procedure is the same as that of an echelon right. (See figure 4-29, page 4-24; figure 4-30, page 4-24; and figure 4-31, page 4-25 for examples of echelon formations with support.)

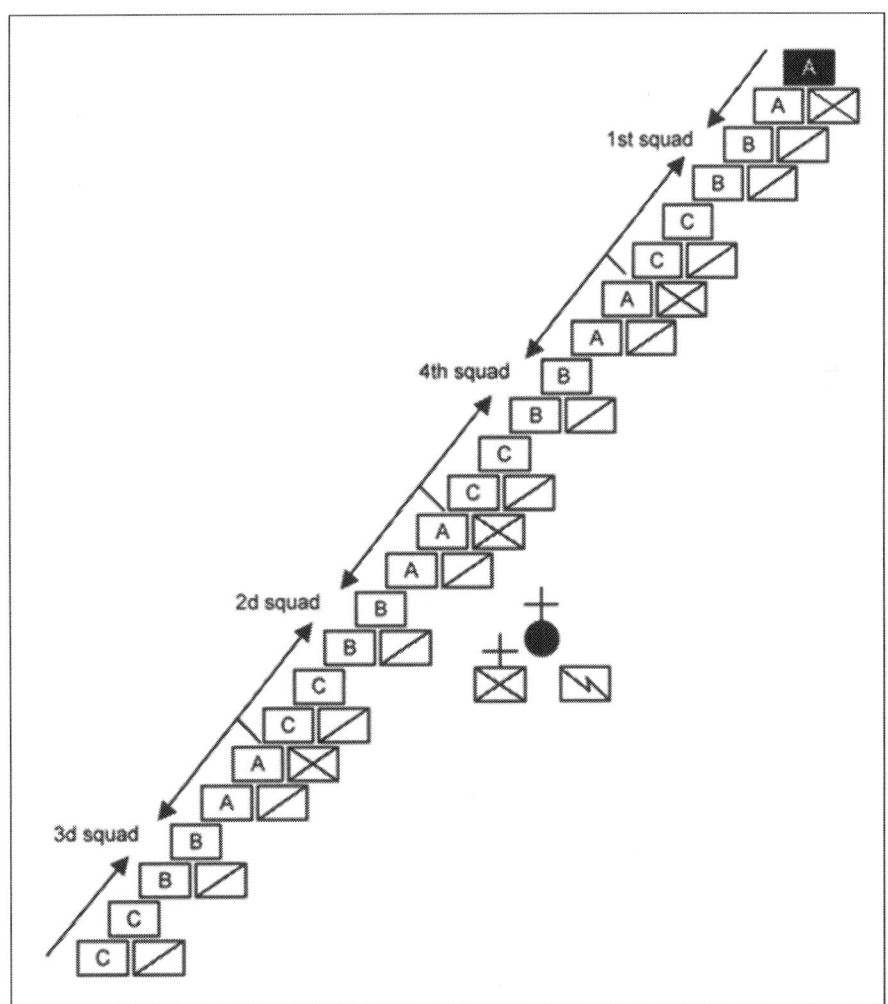

Figure 4-28. Platoon echelon left formation with four squads

Chapter 4

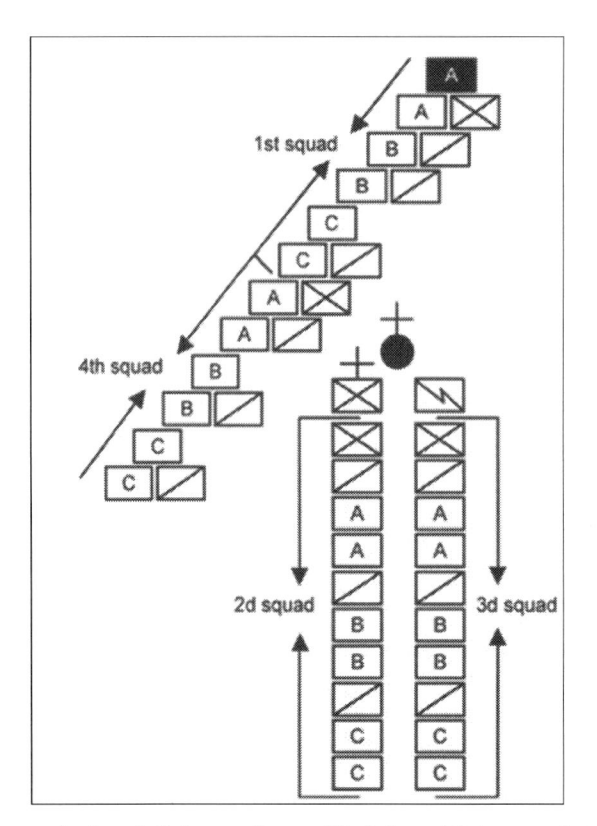

Figure 4-29. Platoon echelon left formation with 2d and 3d squads in general support

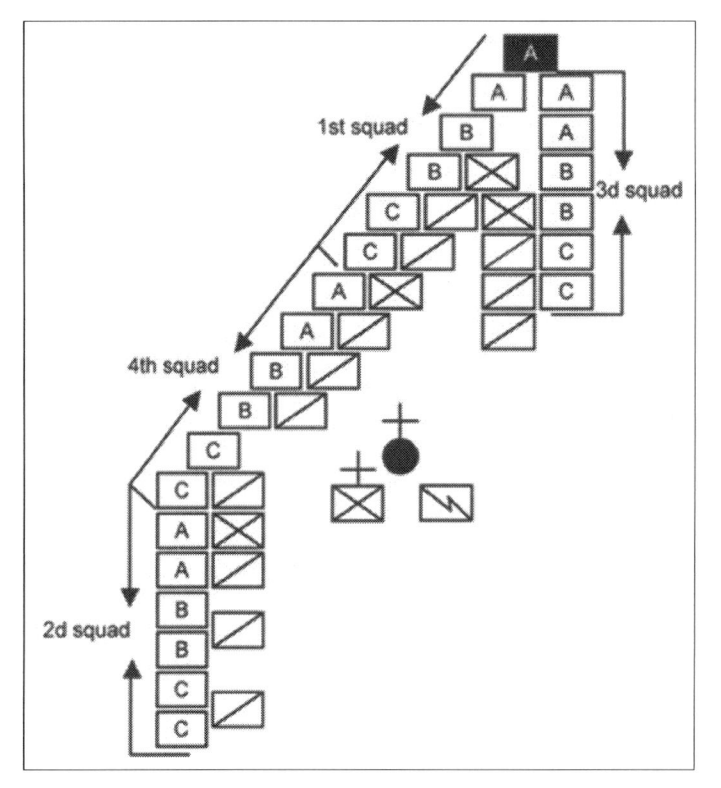

Figure 4-30. Platoon echelon left formation with 2d and 3d squads in lateral support

Control Force Formations

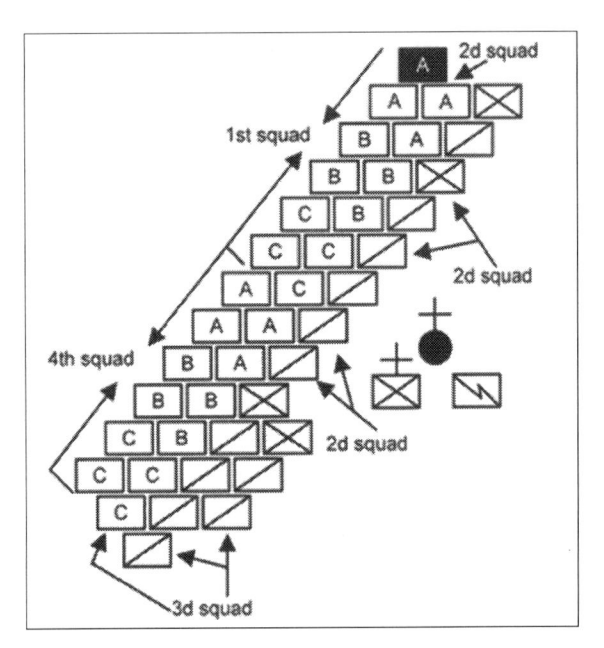

Figure 4-31. Platoon echelon left formation with 2d and 3d squads in direct support

PLATOON WEDGE FORMATION

4-79. The command for forming the platoon wedge formation is "Platoon wedge, move." After the platoon leader's preparatory command, the 1st and 4th squad leaders command, "Follow me." At the same time, the 2d and 3d squad leaders command, "Stand fast." On the platoon leader's command of execution, the 1st and 4th squads move directly to the front. When the last members of the 1st and 4th squads clear the 2d and 3d squads, the 2d and 3d squad leaders command, "Follow me," and move out to the left and right. The 1st squad executes an echelon left on the baseman and the 4th squad executes an echelon right. The 2d squad forms an echelon left on the last man of the 1st squad. The 3d squad forms an echelon right on the last man of the 4th squad. This completes the wedge formation (see figure 4-32). To assemble the platoon, the procedure is the same as that of a platoon line.

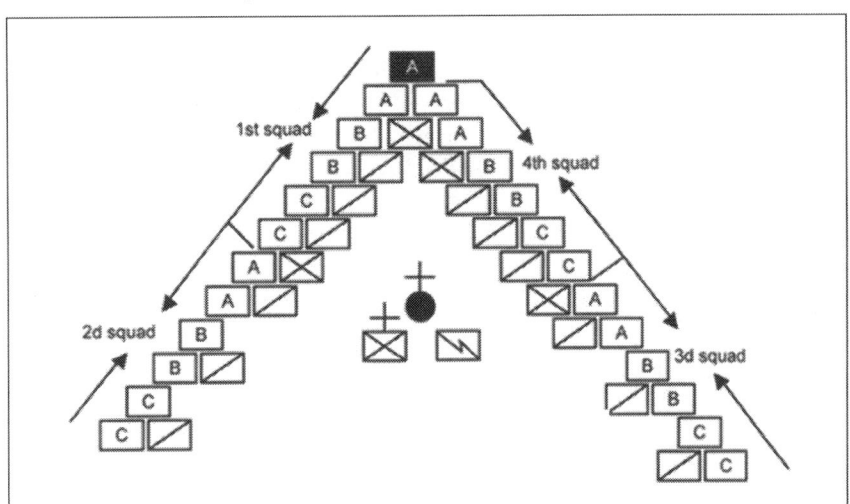

Figure 4-32. Platoon wedge formation with four squads

21 April 2014 ATP 3-39.33 4-25

Chapter 4

Platoon Wedge Formation With General Support

4-80. The command for forming a platoon wedge formation with two squads in support is "Platoon wedge, 2d and 3d squads in support, move." The 1st and 4th squads execute the wedge while the 2d and 3d squads remain in column formation (see figure 4-33).

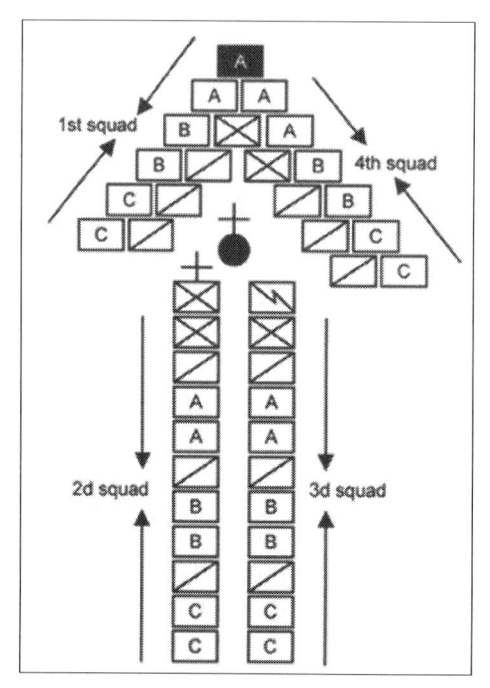

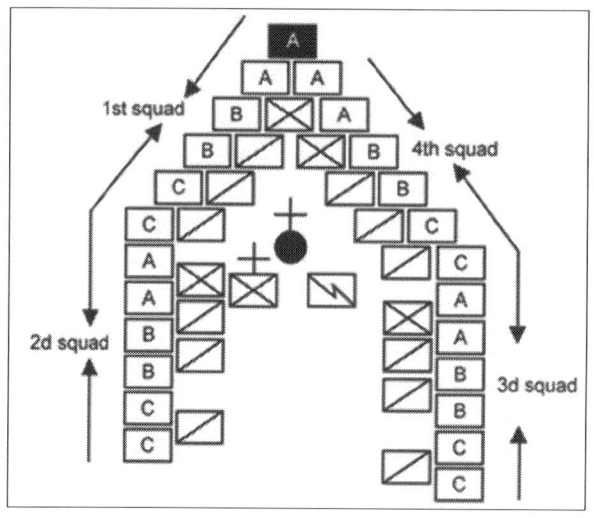

Figure 4-33. Platoon wedge formation with 2d and 3d squads in general support

Platoon Wedge Formation With Lateral Support

4-81. The command for forming a platoon wedge formation with lateral support is "Platoon wedge, 2d and 3d squads in lateral support, move." The 1st and 4th squads execute the wedge while the 2d and 3d squads stand fast. After the 1st and 4th squads have cleared the column, the 2d and 3d squad leaders command, "Follow me," and move out to the left and right. The 2d squad forms a column formation behind the last man of the 1st squad. The 3d squad forms a column formation behind the last man of the 4th squad (see figure 4-34).

Figure 4-34. Platoon wedge formation with 2d and 3d squads in lateral support

4-82. To move the 2d and 3d squads from general to lateral support, the platoon leader commands, "2d and 3d squads, lateral support, move." To have the 2d and 3d squads join the wedge from general or lateral support, the platoon leader commands, "2d and 3d squads, extend the wedge, move." The 2d and 3d squad leaders command, "Follow me," and move out to the left and right to extend the wedge on the 1st and 4th squads.

Platoon Wedge Formation With Direct Support

4-83. The command for forming a platoon wedge with two squads in direct support is "Platoon wedge, 2d and 3d squads in direct support, move." The 1st and 4th squads execute a wedge. The 2d and 3d squads execute a wedge and close in on the leading wedge. The members in the supporting wedge cover the intervals between members in the leading wedge. To do this, the squad and team leaders of the 1st and 4th squads must take two steps to the rear to allow space for the 2d and 3d squads to move into place. After seeing the squad and team leaders move back from the line, the 2d and 3d squad leaders command, "Follow Me," and lead the squads into position (See figure 4-35). To move the 2d and 3d squads back to general support, the platoon leader commands, "2d and 3d squads support, move." Then the 2d and 3d squads move to the general support positions. To assemble a platoon from a platoon wedge with direct support, the procedure is the same as that of a platoon wedge, except that the 2d squad assembles first, followed by the 3d, 1st, and 4th squads.

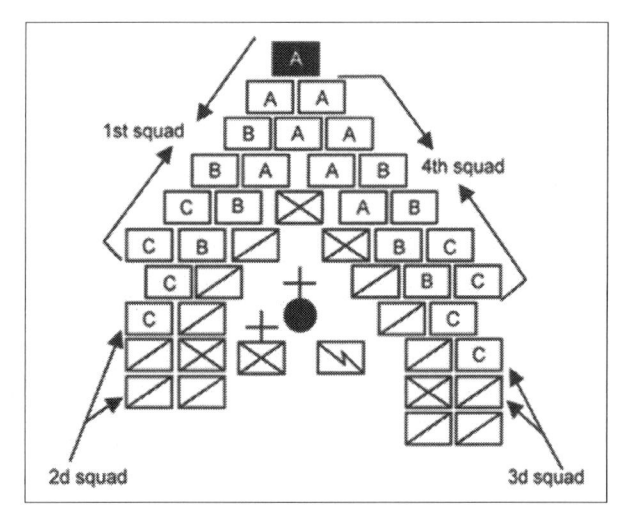

Figure 4-35. Platoon wedge formation with 2d and 3d squads in direct support

Platoon Wedge Formation With One Support Squad

4-84. The command for forming a platoon wedge formation with one squad in support is "Platoon wedge, 3d squad in support, move." The 1st squad moves out and executes a squad wedge. The 2d and 4th squads form echelons left and right on the 1st squad. The 3d squad remains in the column formation.

PLATOON DIAMOND AND CIRCLE FORMATIONS

4-85. The platoon diamond and circle formations are used in open areas or where the crowd may be able to envelop the formation. They are primarily defensive in nature and hard to maneuver. The decision concerning which formation to use is based on the ability of the platoon to perform them. The command for having a platoon form in a diamond or circle formation is "Platoon diamond [or circle], move." On the command of execution, the 1st squad leader moves the baseman to the location indicated by the platoon leader. The baseman becomes the 12 o'clock position. The 1st squad lines up to the left of the baseman covering the 9 to 12 o'clock positions. The 4th squad aligns themselves to the right of the baseman covering the 12 to 3 o'clock positions. The 3d squad aligns itself covering the 3 to 6 o'clock positions. The 2d squad aligns itself covering the 6 to 9 o'clock positions.

4-86. To assemble a platoon from a platoon diamond or circle formation, the headquarters element uses the same procedures as that of a line formation. The 1st squad leads the platoon back to the AA followed by the 2d, 3d, and 4th squads. The squads fall into a column formation as they file back to the AA.

COMPANY FORMATIONS

4-87. When a company commander orders his company into control force formations from a column, they move to the left near the head of the column so that they are seen by the platoon leaders. The commander then faces the company. As the commander gives the preparatory command, they point to where they want the formation. If no location is indicated, the company forms immediately in front of the lead platoon.

4-88. For relieving elements in place, a platoon leader within a company formation may rotate the squads to give them rest.

COMPANY LINE FORMATIONS

4-89. A company commander has several options of line formations for the company. These include line in depth and line in mass with the various methods of support used.

Company Line in Depth Formation

4-90. The command for forming a company line in depth formation (see figure 4-36) is "Company line in depth, move." After the company commander's preparatory command, each platoon leader gives the command, "Platoon line." The squad leaders follow with the commands to the squads to form the platoon line. On the command of execution, each platoon establishes a platoon line immediately to its front.

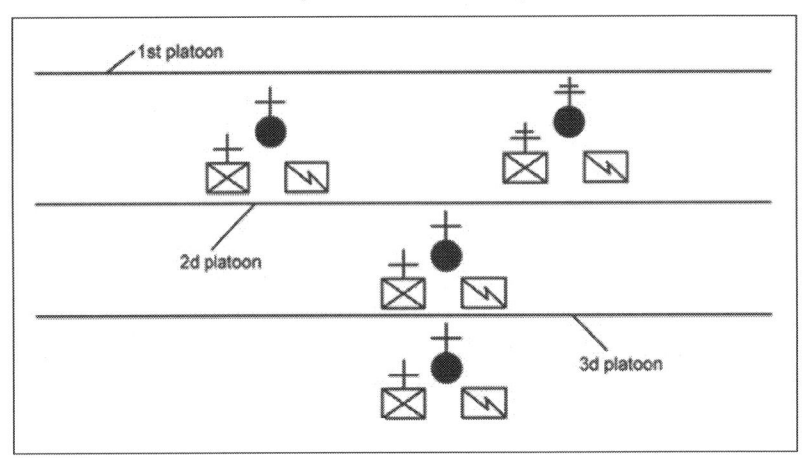

Figure 4-36. Company line in depth formation

4-91. If the commander wants a more formidable formation, they command, "2d platoon, direct support, move." The squad and team leaders from the 1st platoon take two steps backward. The 2d platoon moves forward and covers the intervals between the members of the lead platoon. The platoon leader of the 3d platoon then moves his platoon forward to occupy the position formerly held by the 2d platoon.

4-92. If the 3d platoon is called on to support the company line, it moves forward and takes up a position directly behind the 2d platoon in the same manner. Platoon leaders and PSGs help each other in controlling the company.

Company Line-in-Mass Formation

4-93. The command for forming a company line-in-mass formation is "Company line in mass, move" (see figure 4-37). The company line in mass is the same as a company line with both platoons in direct support. Instead of forming it in stages, the company commander indicates the desire for this formation in the initial command. The platoons each form a line, and the 2d and 3d platoons close on the 1st platoon without further command.

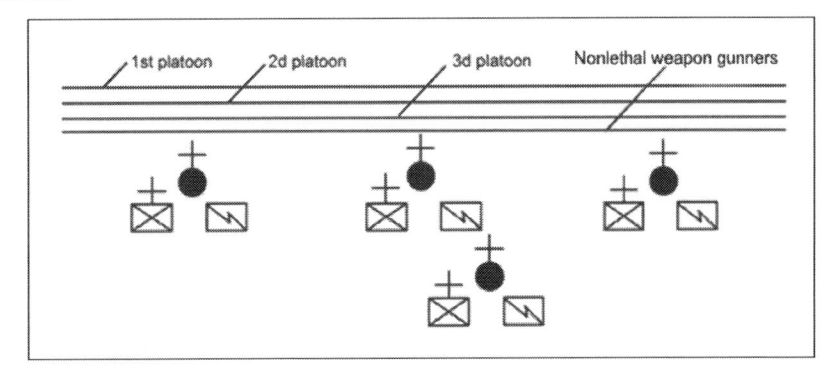

Figure 4-37. Company line-in-mass formation

Company Line Formations With Support

4-94. In company formations, the 1st platoon usually forms the lead element and the 2d and 3d platoons provide support (see figure 4-38; figure 4-39; and figure 4-40, page 4-30). The support platoons can be employed in the same manner as the support squads in platoon formations. One platoon can be relieved from the lead element by another platoon, while in formation, by having a support platoon pass through the lead platoon.

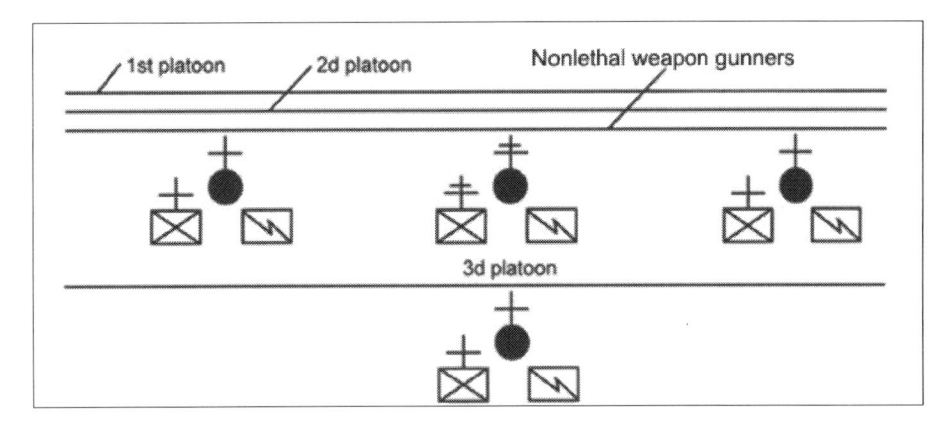

Figure 4-38. Company line mass formation with one platoon in depth

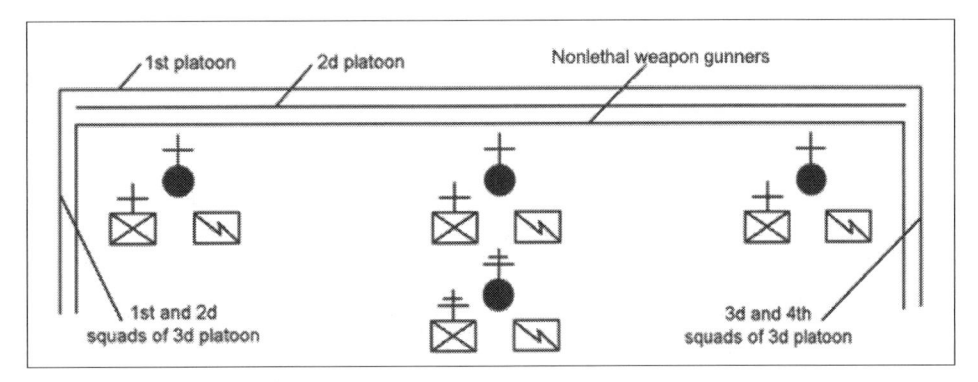

Figure 4-39. Company line-in-mass formation with one platoon in lateral support

Chapter 4

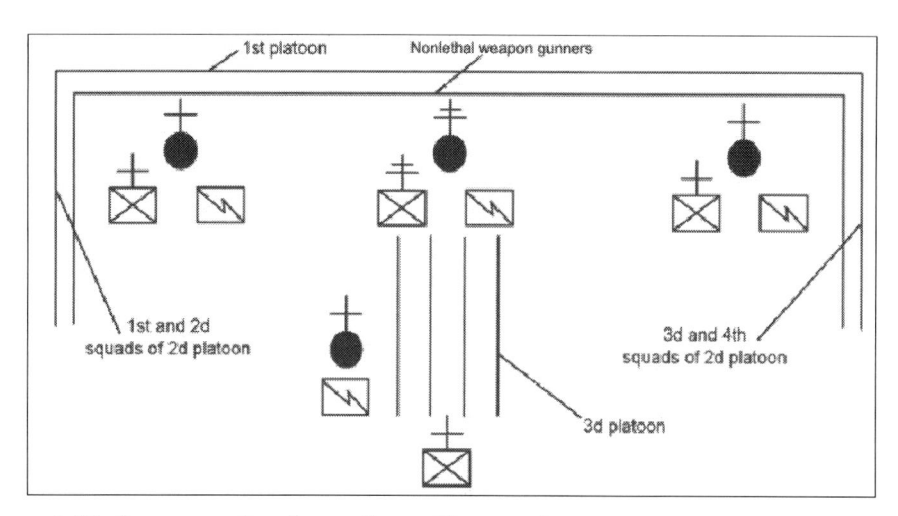

Figure 4-40. Company line formation with one platoon in lateral support and one platoon in general support

COMPANY ECHELONS AND WEDGE FORMATIONS

4-95. Company echelons (see figure 4-41; figure 4-42; figure 4-43; and figure 4-44, page 4-32) and company wedge formations (see figure 4-45, page 4-32; figure 4-46, page 4-33; and figure 4-47, page 4-33) are formed in the same manner and with the same variations as the company line formation. A company assembles from a crowd control formation in the same manner as a platoon or a squad does. However, due to the size of company formations, the commander must consider the area that the company is operating in when assembling the company. If following the guidelines of platoon assembly, the commander will have no difficulty. When assembling the company, the commander takes a position to the rear of the formation and commands, "Company assemble." The platoon leaders take charge of the respective platoons. Usually, the 3d platoon assembles first, just behind the formation. After the 3d platoon is assembled, the 2d platoon assembles in front of the 3d platoon and the 1st platoon assembles in front of the 2d. All platoons assemble facing the commander. The 2d and 3d platoons then dress with the 1st platoon. As each platoon is assembled, they are ordered to port arms by the platoon leader to await further orders from the commander. If four platoons are used, the 4th platoon assembles first.

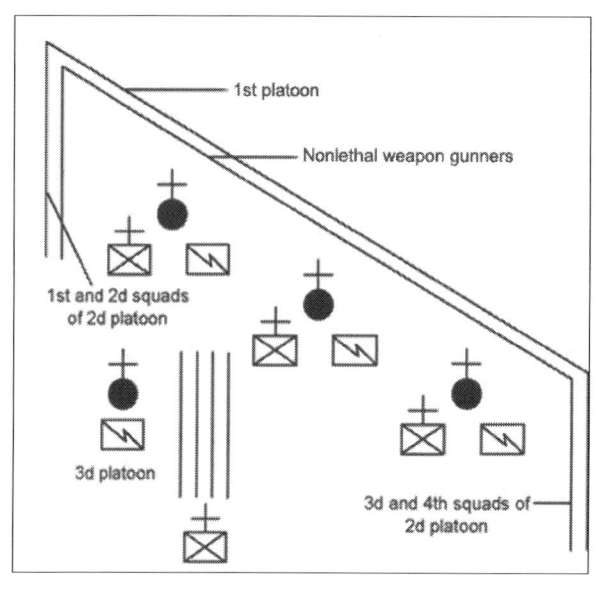

Figure 4-41. Company echelon right formation with one platoon in lateral support and one platoon in general support

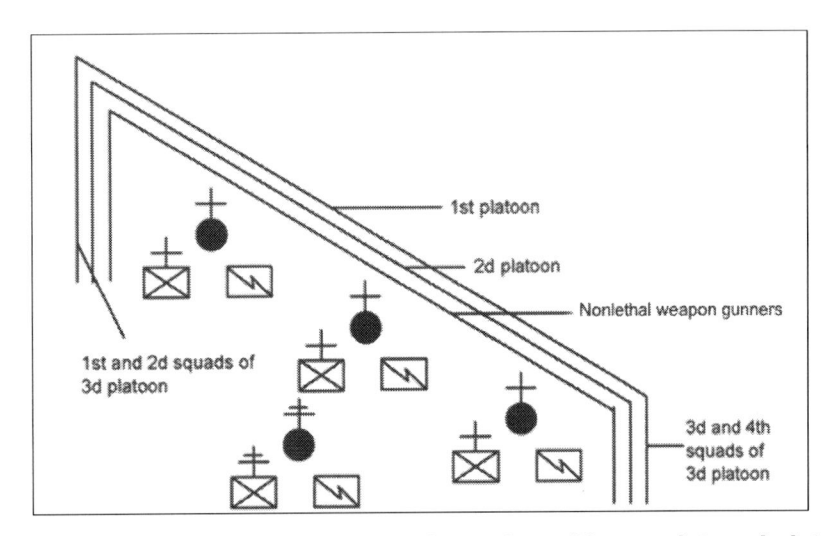

Figure 4-42. Company echelon right in mass formation with one platoon in lateral support

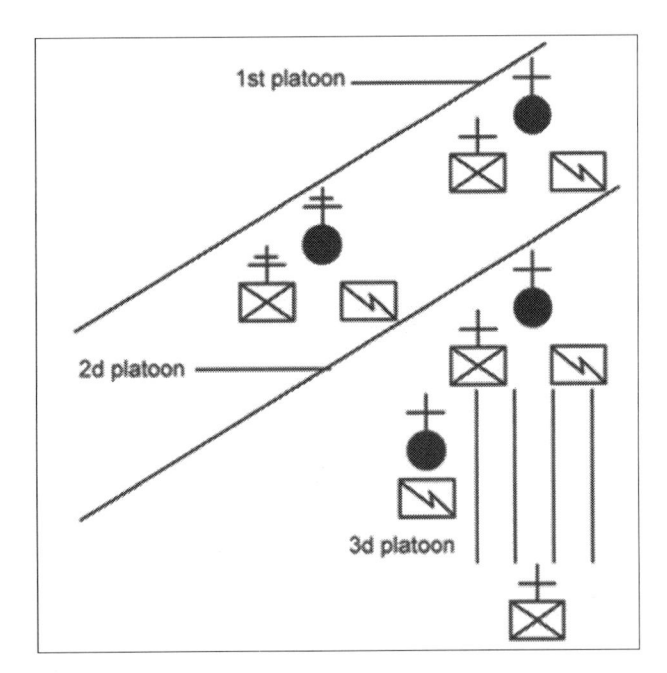

Figure 4-43. Company echelon left formation with one platoon in general support

Chapter 4

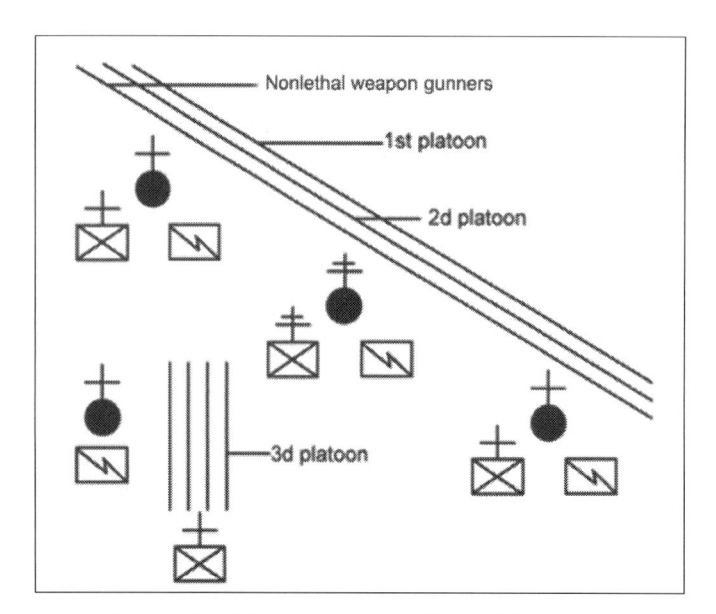

Figure 4-44. Company echelon right in mass formation with one platoon in general support

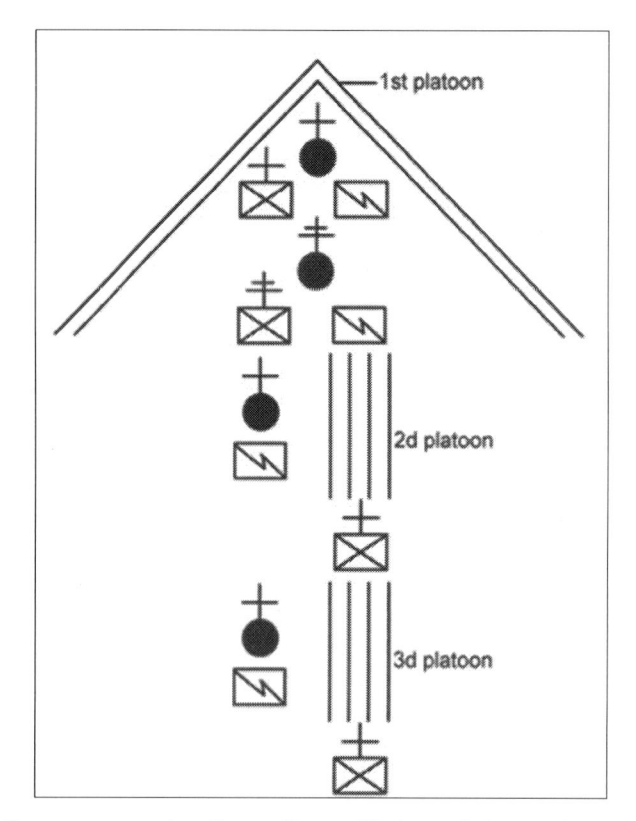

Figure 4-45. Company wedge formation with two platoons in general support

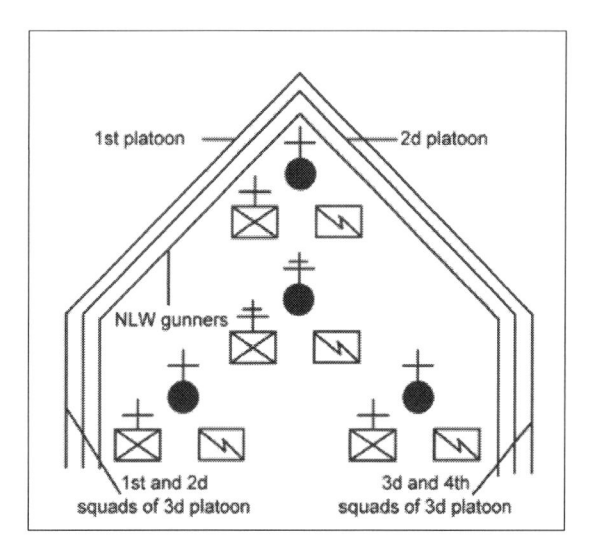

Figure 4-46. Company wedge formation with one platoon in lateral support

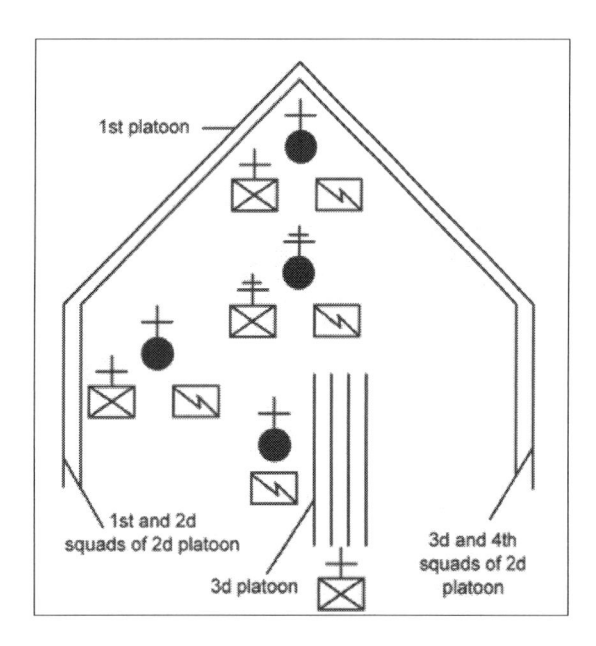

Figure 4-47. Company wedge formation with one platoon in lateral support and one platoon in general support

FORMATIONS WITH VEHICLES

4-96. The commands for vehicles and foot troops are the same as those for foot troops alone. Because of the additional noise and distances involved, the company commander gives the hand-and-arm signal for the line. The command and the signal apply to the lead platoon only. The other platoons remain in general support until further directed (see figure 4-48, page 4-34; figure 4-49, page 4-34; figure 4-50, page 4-35; figure 4-51, page 4-35; figure 4-52, page 4-35; and figure 4-53, page 4-36).

Chapter 4

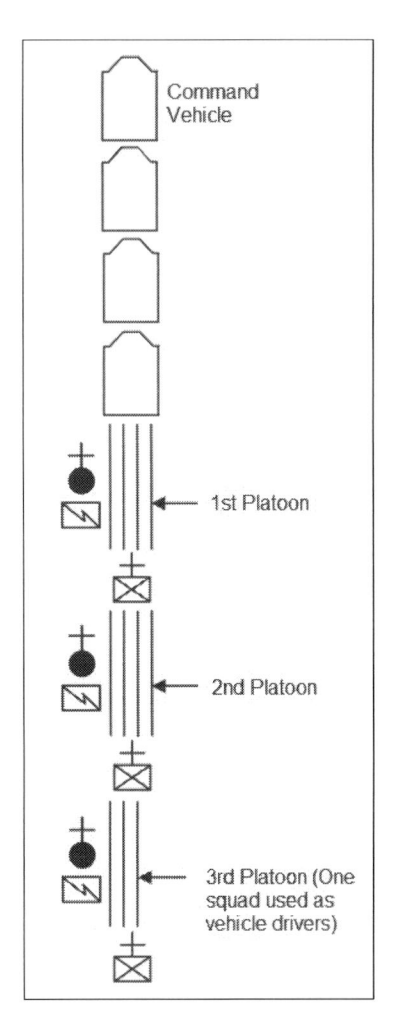

Figure 4-48. Company column formation with vehicles

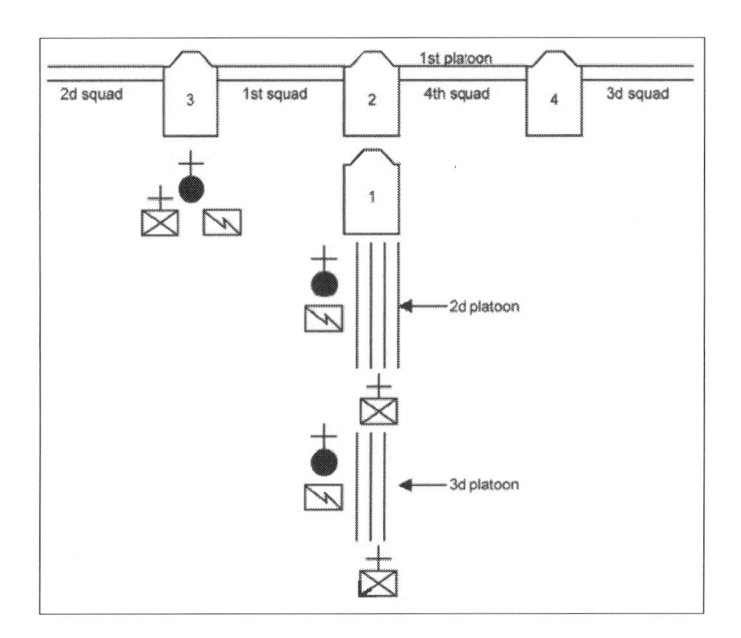

Figure 4-49. Company line formation with vehicles and two platoons in general support

Control Force Formations

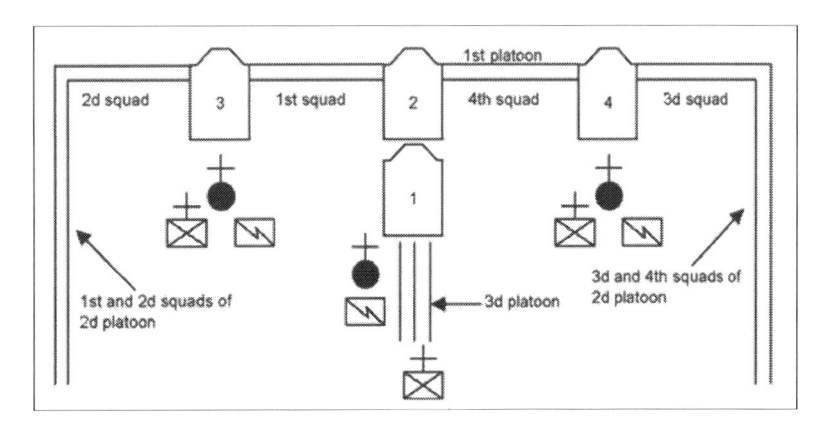

Figure 4-50. Company line formation with vehicles, one platoon in lateral support and one platoon in general support

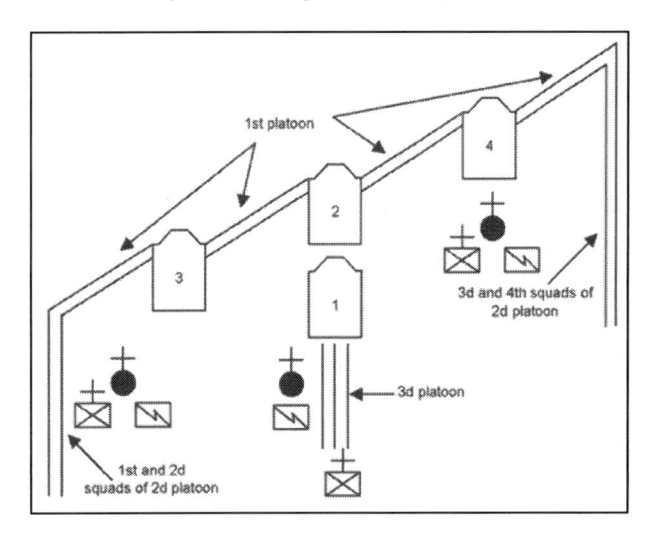

Figure 4-51. Company echelon left formation with vehicles, one platoon in lateral support and one platoon in general support

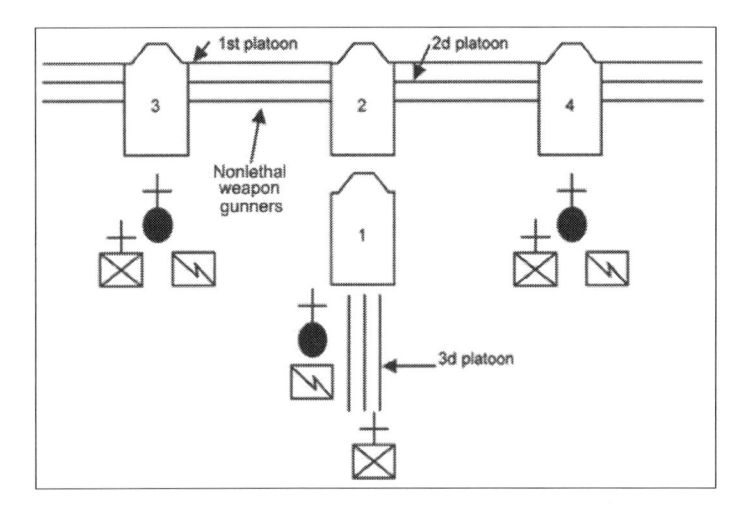

Figure 4-52. Company line-in-mass formation with vehicles and one platoon in general support

Chapter 4

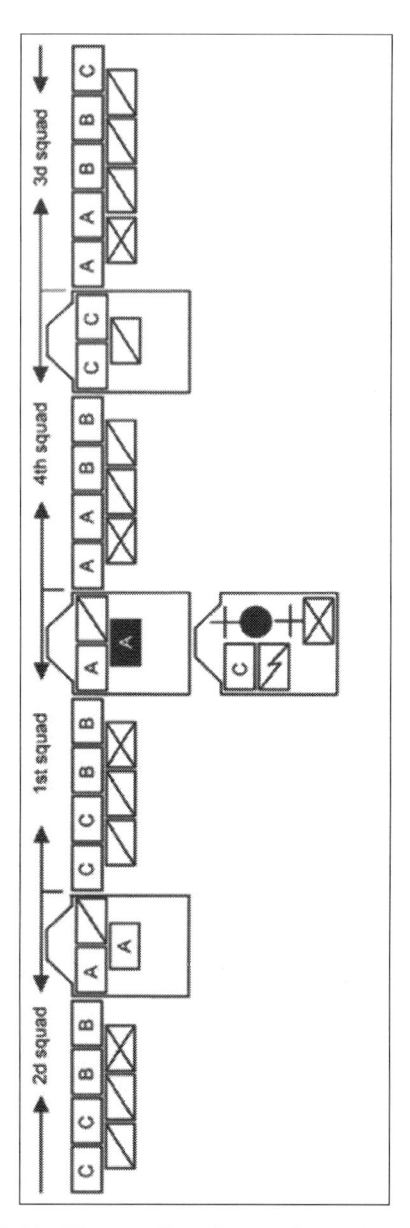

Figure 4-53. Platoon line formation with vehicles

4-97. The motor section moves out with vehicle number two moving to the right. Vehicle number two passes the lead vehicle and establishes the position for the center of the line. At the same time, the 3d and 4th vehicles swing out to the left and right. They form to the left and right and slightly to the rear of vehicle number two. The 1st and 4th squads of the lead platoon then move forward and form lines to the left and right, on the front end of vehicle number two. As soon as the troops are in position, the 3d and 4th vehicles close in on the squads and tighten the formation. The 2d and 3d squads of the lead platoon then form a line to the left and right of the 3d and 4th vehicles to complete the company line. The command vehicle (vehicle number one) takes up a position behind the line where the commander can direct and control the unit. The 2d and 3d platoons move forward and are used in general, lateral, or direct support. In some instances, foot troops move into position first and vehicles join the formation, as needed.

4-98. To form a company echelon or a company wedge with vehicles, the company follows the same procedures used for company formations without vehicles. Vehicles are moved into the appropriate positions using procedures similar to those used for a company line.

4-99. To assemble troops and vehicles, the command vehicle moves to a position behind the formation. The commander faces the formation and gives the vehicle section the signal for assembly. Immediately, the vehicles return to the proper positions in column formation behind the command vehicle while the troops stand fast. The second in command then assembles the troops in the usual manner.

ADDITIONAL FORMATIONS

4-100. Along with the five basic control force formations (line, echelon, wedge, diamond, and circle), there are additional formations that are utilized for specific situations. It is up to the leader on the ground to determine which formations, or variations of those formations are necessary and best suits the situation that the control force encounters. Two additional formations that can be used by the control force are junction check and open formation.

JUNCTION CHECK

4-101. A junction check is basically the modification of a line formation where one end of the line turns inward to a 90 degree angle. This formation is used to see down a cross street, alley, or area around a structure such as a building. To conduct a junction check, the leader of the element that is currently in a line formation gives the command, "Junction check, right [or left]." On the command of execution, the element on the opposite side of the direction given turns inward (staying on line) 90° to the main line. The element is now facing down the direction given by the leader and can observe the junction (cross street, alley, or side of building). Figure 4-54 shows the junction check with a platoon line.

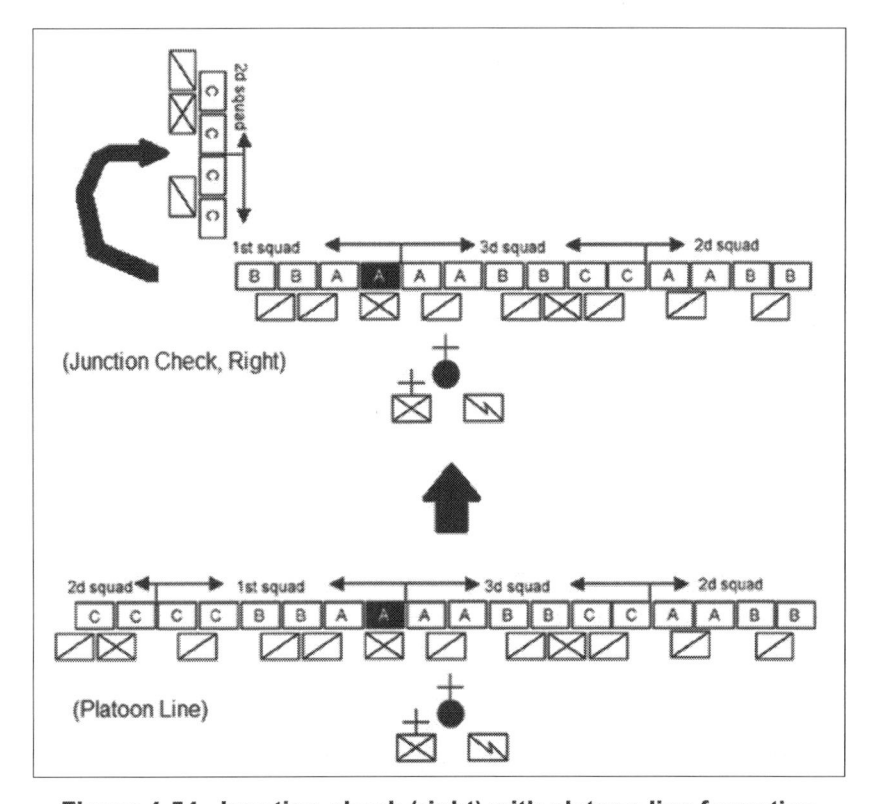

Figure 4-54. Junction check (right) with platoon line formation

OPEN FORMATION

4-102. The open formation is utilized when there is no immediate threat to the control force, when the element wants to move more quickly without staying in a tight line or other formation, or when the control force wants to cover more area and give off a larger presence to the crowd. To put the element into the open formation, the leader commands, commands, "Platoon [or another element], open." The open order

Chapter 4

can be given to any element. To transform into the open formation, internal elements (for example, squads), remaining on line, stagger behind or in front another element. The individual Soldiers spread out to a distance of one baton plus six inches between them. Figure 4-55 shows a platoon line formation that has moved into the open formation. In this example, 1st squad stays in place, 2d squad forms in front, and 3d squad forms behind 1st squad. The command element moves rearward to allow space for the formation, and remains behind the main element.

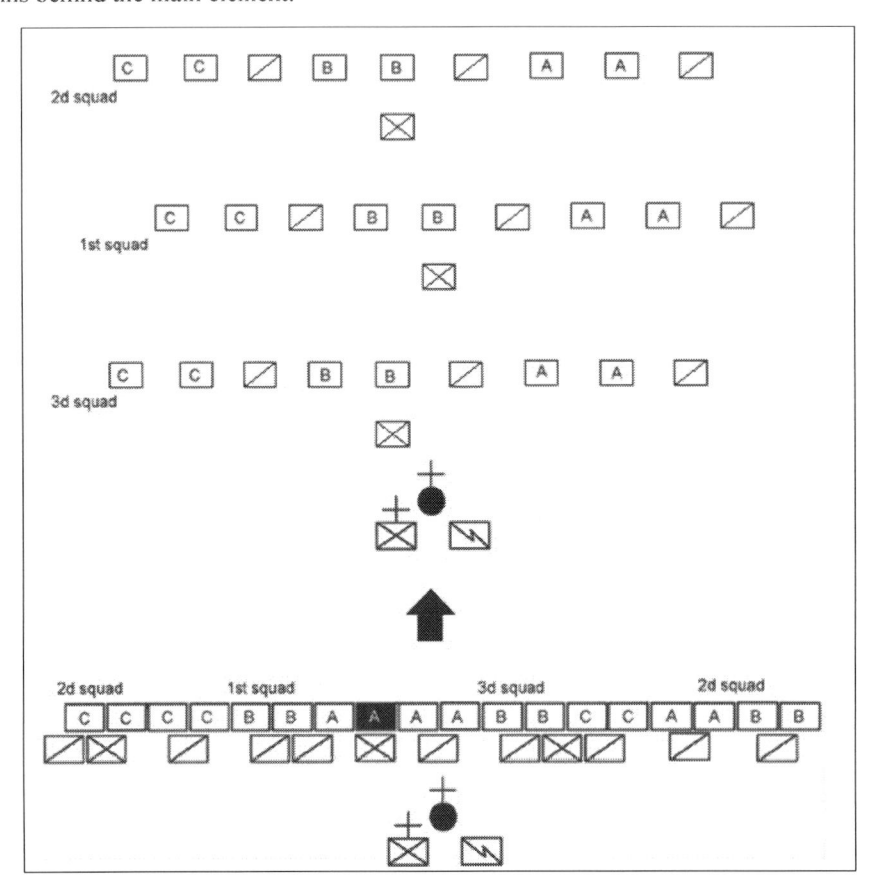

Figure 4-55. Open formation from a platoon line formation

Chapter 5
Confinement Facilities

Civil disturbances do not always occur in large open areas where the size of the responding force or the type of formation employed is not hampered by a lack of space. In the military confinement environment, inmate disturbances often occur in small, closed areas, such as an inmate's housing unit, a gymnasium, a dining facility, or a chapel where maneuver space and equipment limit the size of the element that is employed. The layout of each facility is different and presents its own unique problems when employing forces. This chapter covers the use of small military police teams, forced cell move teams (FCMTs), and the formations used to move an unruly inmate from one cell to another. Small generic riot control formations are discussed to provide the commander with a basic employment option that they can tailor to the facility to enable them to regain control of the affected area. The use of nonlethal munitions and RCAs are incorporated into this discussion as well.

CROWD DYNAMICS

5-1. Within a confinement facility, inmates can be of various backgrounds and cultures. Inmates usually form groups based on these factors, but also based on such things as gang or group affiliation, protection needs, or shared ideas and beliefs. Disturbances in these facilities occur for various reasons and to different degrees of severity and size. Sometimes different groups of inmates with opposing views clash. The most severe, and usually the most dangerous, disturbance is when the majority of inmates come together and riot against the facility and its cadre. In confinement facility disturbances, inmates employ a number of tactics to resist control or achieve goals. These tactics may be unplanned or planned and nonviolent or violent. When a disturbance carries many purposes, it is likely that tactics are well planned.

NONVIOLENT TACTICS

5-2. Nonviolent tactics range from name calling to building barricades. Inmates may attempt to distract control force members by shouting at or ridiculing them or by using abusive language, obscene remarks, taunts, and jeers. The inmates' goals are to anger and demoralize the control force. They also want authorities to take actions that may later be exploited as acts of brutality.

VIOLENT TACTICS

5-3. Violent crowd tactics used by inmates are often extremely destructive and can include physical attacks on cadre, other inmates, and property. Use of violent tactics is limited only by the attitudes and ingenuity of the inmates, leader training, and the materials available to them. Inmates often commit violence with crude homemade weapons. If unplanned violence occurs, inmates will use mops, brooms, chairs, beds, or whatever else is on hand as weapons of violence. During planned violent disturbances, inmates can easily conceal makeshift weapons or tools to use against the control force. Inmates often erect barricades to impede troop movement or to prevent the control force from entering certain areas or buildings. Inmates can be expected to vent emotions on individuals (cadre or inmates), the control force, equipment, and institution's property. Inmates direct potentially dangerous items like carts, barrels, liquids, and burning material at the control force.

Chapter 5

GRIEVANCE PROTEST

5-4. A grievance protest may be organized as a riot. However, under normal circumstances, a riot of this type is not of an extremely violent nature. It may turn violent when leaders attempt to exploit any successes or weaknesses found in the control force.

UNORGANIZED RIOTS

5-5. Unorganized riots are characterized as being spontaneous in nature. However, they could be exploited and diverted by leaders at any subsequent stage of the riot, turning it into a different type. They may begin as an isolated assault against authority figures, or acts of civil disobedience. Under determined leadership, an unorganized riot could change to an organized riot.

MULTIPLE RIOTS

5-6. Multiple riots may happen when a disturbance occurs in one area of the confinement facility, causing others to riot in the areas. To control this situation with only one riot control force available, the force commander should first subdue the most violent riot. At the same time, he should employ some of his control forces to contain the other riots until the main control force is able to move to those locations to subdue them.

CADRE BEHAVIOR

5-7. The cadre is susceptible to crowd behavior. They become emotionally stimulated during tense confrontation with unruly and violent inmates. Commanders must be aware of the mood and attitude of the crowd and its effect on the control force cadre. To counteract the effects of crowd behavior on the cadre, the commanders must institute rigorous training and firm and effective leadership. This training must include a complete awareness and understanding of the use of force and the commander's intent. These are all necessary to offset the effect of crowd contagion or the control force as a second crowd effect upon the control force. Even with the best training and leadership, control force members must exercise individual and collective restraint.

PLANNING

5-8. Planning includes the preparation and training conducted before a crisis occurs. The purpose of planning is to have plans and standing operating procedures (SOPs) in place so that the cadre may react to an emergency and successfully contain and neutralize the situation. The planning process includes plan development, information collection, and training.

Note. Information collection is essential for the successful containment, neutralization, or prevention of a riot within a confinement facility.

5-9. During the planning process, leaders must be aware of the potential risks, as well as the level of risk, involved in quelling disturbances within a confinement facility. Careful planning minimizes collateral damage and risks to control force members and hostages. When a disturbance in a confinement facility occurs, leaders need to determine and disseminate key pieces of information, these include—
- Location of the disturbance.
- Estimated number of participants or rioters.
- Accessibility of weapons, tools, and cleaning supplies.
- The inmates' military training.
- If there is a hostage situation.

Note. During planning leaders must consider that the crowd may become more combative with the arrival of a control force.

5-10. Once the control force team has been alerted to a disturbance within the confinement facility, leaders further develop a plan to fit the situation. Troop leading procedures and METT-TC come into play; however, in these situations, time is a factor and the team must act quickly. Having quality plans and SOPs, and with previous training, the control force team is able to move in quickly to deal with any situation that may occur.

5-11. Based on the analysis of the factors from paragraph 5-9, the commander makes an estimate of the situation. This estimate must be as thorough as time permits. Using the estimate, the commander considers COAs, selects NLWs and RCAs to be used, and determines the need for engineer support. In choosing a COA, the following factors of the disturbance are considered:
- Number of hostages.
- Number of inmates holding the hostages.
- Who the leader is.
- Attitude and demeanor of the rioters.
- Location of the riot.
  - Inside areas of the confinement facility, such as the dining facility, work site, or housing wing.
  - Outside areas of the confinement facility, such as the exercise or work areas.
- Accessibility of weapons or material to make weapons.
- Accessibility of chemicals, such as cleaning supplies.

5-12. The use of NLW and nonlethal munitions must be considered when developing plans. There must be strict accountability and control of RCAs, employment, and other appropriate nonlethal means (such as high-pressure water hoses).

USE OF CHEMICAL IRRITANTS

5-13. The use of chemical irritants can be a valuable nonlethal tool for control force leadership to consider during the planning phase. These chemical irritants can drive a threat from an established, enclosed position or deny the rioters access to a certain area without long-lasting effects to those involved. The proper use of chemical irritants may prevent the control force from having to enter a dangerous area; however, improper use can cause property damage, injury, or death.

5-14. The installation commander authorizes the use of chemical irritants after the control force leader determines the type and dosage. The confinement facility's SOP needs to outline the procedures for securing authorization and provides guidance to help the control force leader make decisions. The confinement facility commandant/commander should inform the installation commander of the situation, since the installation commander is ultimately responsible. Team members must be aware of how chemical irritants affect personnel and plan accordingly. Inmates not involved must be removed from the area and the chemical cloud's path. The fire department and emergency medical services should be on standby during operations involving chemicals.

Pepper Irritant

5-15. The pepper irritant receives its name from varieties of the capsicum plant that it is made from. The active ingredient, is extracted from the plant and micro-pulverized to make the irritant. It is neither a chemical nor a gas, but an all-natural organic substance. It is effective against individuals who are emotionally disturbed or under the influence of drugs or alcohol. There is a very small part of the population that are not affected by pepper spray (less than 1 percent). Pepper spray is often used to divert the threat from making or continuing an assault. OC does not cause permanent damage. Its effects last 30 to 60 minutes after individuals are placed in fresh air.

5-16. Pepper spray can have various effects on people, which include the following:
- Swelling of mucous membranes and the upper respiratory system; however, it does not shut down the system.
- Burning (intense) and discoloration (bright red) of exposed skin.

- Dilating the capillaries.
- Swelling of the eyelids.
- Burning and involuntary closing of the eyes.
- Coughing uncontrollably.
- Gagging.
- Gasping for air.
- Losing strength and coordination (temporarily).

Dissemination of Chemical Irritants

5-17. Careful consideration for the dissemination of chemical irritants must be taken by leaders and Soldiers when the approval for use has been given. There are six methods of dissemination discussed in the following paragraphs.

Pyrotechnic Method

5-18. In the pyrotechnic method of dissemination, the chemical irritant is placed in a canister with an inert material that is ignited when the device is activated. The agent is then carried into the air on the smoke particles of the inert material.

5-19. There are some disadvantages when using a pyrotechnic device indoors. These disadvantages are that the device—
- May cause a fire.
- Has a very slow saturation time (40 to 45 seconds to burn completely).
- Can be thrown back by the threat, even while burning.

Bursting Method

5-20. In the bursting method of dissemination, the irritant and an inert powder are placed in a saw-toothed canister. After a small detonation, the canister splits and expels the irritant in a cloud. The bursting method has both advantages and disadvantages, which include—
- Advantages—
  - There is no risk of fire.
  - There is no risk of the canister being thrown back.
  - The contents disseminate quickly.
  - The canister is effective, easy to carry, and easy to control.
- Disadvantages—
  - There is a slight possibility of fragmentation when detonated.
  - The fuse head may separate from the canister.
  - Only 50 to 90 percent of the irritant may be disseminated.
  - The direction of the cloud formation depends on where the device is detonated.

Aerosol Method

5-21. In the aerosol method of dissemination, the irritant is suspended in an inert liquid that is located in the rear portion of the device. When the projectile penetrates the structure, the rear portion splits open and the irritant is disseminated in a mist. The aerosol method is most appropriate for tactical operations when chemical irritants are used before entry. The aerosol method has both advantages and disadvantages, which include—
- Advantages—
  - Easily carried.
  - Easily deployed from various ammunition (37 millimeter, 40 millimeter, and 12 gauge).
  - Contents are dispersed quickly.
  - Easily controlled and accurate (fin-stabilized rounds).

- Disadvantages—
  - Can cause injury to individuals if fired at close range.
  - Can damage property if it strikes a weak portion.

Projectile Method

5-22. Chemical-containing projectiles can be very effective when used correctly. A Soldier must know which projectile to use in each unique situation.
- **Thirty-seven-millimeter projectile**. A 37-millimeter projectile can incapacitate individuals in an enclosed area of 4,500 cubic feet. It can penetrate the following:
  - A sheet of 3/4-inch thick plywood at 25 yards.
  - An automobile windshield at 33 yards.
  - A hollow-core door at 58 yards.
- **Forty-millimeter projectile**. A 40-millimeter projectile is more effective at greater ranges than a 37-millimeter projectile because of its rifled bore. It can incapacitate individuals in an enclosed area of 4,500 cubic feet. It can penetrate the following:
  - A sheet of 1 inch thick plywood at 10 yards.
  - An automobile windshield at 55 yards.
  - A hollow-core door at 109 yards.
- **Twelve-gauge projectile**. A 12-gauge projectile can be loaded into a shotgun with no modifications to the weapon. It can be fired as a single round, or it can be magazine-fed. The 12-gauge projectile can incapacitate individuals in an enclosed area of 1,000 cubic feet. The angle at which the projectile strikes the barrier can affect its penetration capability. It can penetrate the following:
  - A sheet of 3/4-inch plywood at 33 yards.
  - An automobile windshield at 33 yards.
  - A hollow-core door at 100 yards.

Fogging Method

5-23. The irritant is suspended in a fogging solution and dispersed with a fogging machine. It is not recommended for tactical operations. The fogging method has its advantages and disadvantages, which include—
- Advantages—
  - Produces enough chemical irritant to cover an enclosed area of 100,000 cubic feet in 26 seconds.
  - Disseminates quickly.
  - Provides high-volume capabilities.
  - Very effective for riot control and crowd dispersal.
- Disadvantages—
  - Noisy.
  - Cumbersome.

Multipurpose Grenade Method

5-24. A multipurpose grenade can be hand-thrown or launched from a shotgun with an adapter. It has an extended shelf life of 6 years and an adjustable fuse delay of 2 to 5 seconds. The irritant is located in the cylinder portion of the device and is forced out the bottom of the grenade upon detonation.

Chapter 5

> **WARNING**
>
> A multipurpose grenade deployed incorrectly could result in injury. Safety rules should be observed at all times.

RECORD OF EVENTS

5-25. Reporting procedures for serious incidents should be included in planning. A record of events must be initiated to provide a basis for the preparation and submission of a formal report to higher headquarters. At a minimum, this needs to include the following:
- Time the incident was reported and by whom.
- Time the incident was reported to the facility commander.
- Time the control force was assembled.
- Time the control force entered the facility.
- Weather conditions as they relate to the use of RCAs.
- Number of cadre and inmates injured or killed, including how they were injured or killed and the medical attention given to them.
- Time the operation was completed.
- Time the riot control force restored order.

EQUIPMENT

5-26. Leaders must consider what equipment is to be used by the control force. This information needs to be clearly established in the unit's SOP. The recommended basic riot gear used by the control force in a confinement facility includes—
- Riot baton.
- Riot shield.
- Helmet with face shield.
- Groin protector.
- Body Armor.
- Leather gloves.
- Shin protection.

CONTROL FORCE FORMATIONS

5-27. The five basic formations for civil disturbance operations are the line, wedge, echelon, diamond, and circle. In the correctional environment the basic formations for disturbances are the line, wedge, or echelon with apprehension teams in support. Generally, the diamond and circle formations are not used in the correctional environment. The minimum size force that the commander should consider is an augmented platoon, with a two-to-one advantage over the rioters.

5-28. Correctional facility cadre must be proficient in all riot control formations. These are usually trained at the squad level and above, but performed by a platoon or company-size unit. Squad line, echelon left, echelon right, and wedge formations form the basis for platoon and company formations. Each squad must be adept in the basic formations before practicing in platoon-size or larger formations. In the correctional environment, the support platoon plays a key role by supporting the control formation with apprehension and equipment teams. See chapter 4 for an in-depth discussion on civil disturbance formations.

SPECIALIZED TEAMS

5-29. Situations and events during a civil disturbance situation within a confinement facility can vary greatly. Due to the confined space within a facility, the employment of specialized teams (extraction teams and FCMTs) requires careful planning and procedures to be in place. The members that make up these teams need to be thoroughly trained and confident in duties and abilities. These specialized teams, team responsibilities, and the signals used (verbal and hand-and-arm) need to be clear in the unit's SOP. Due to various sizes and designs of confinement facilities, as well as a unit's personnel and experience, specialized teams can be of various sizes and responsibilities. The following discussion on the two primary specialized teams is general in nature, and is only a recommendation for some of the basic requirements. Teams need to be flexible to meet the needs of the commander and the situation.

Extraction Team

5-30. Extraction teams give the control force the ability to remove inmates from the crowd. Inmates identified as leaders or agitators and inmates that are injured or no longer want to resist can be extracted from the crowd. Extraction teams can also be used to enter confined areas where the formation cannot operate.

5-31. A typical extraction team consists of eight members and one leader. The nine-Soldier team has four shield holders, two nonlethal gunners, two apprehension and search members, and a squad leader. The squad leader controls the movement of the team and assists the team in exiting the control formation. They maintain communications with the formation and coordinate the team's operations with the formation. The squad leader also ensures that the team uses the minimum amount of force necessary to extract inmates.

5-32. The extraction team may deploy through the middle of the formation or from around either of the flanks. The team should be deployed within a distance of approximately 10 meters so that the formation can still provide immediate support. If the extraction team is deployed farther than 10 meters, the formation must advance to close the gap.

5-33. The extraction team exits the formation in two columns; shield holders in the first and second ranks, nonlethal gunners in the third rank, apprehension and search members in the fourth rank, and the leader last. Team members grip the shoulder or equipment of the member in front of them. The shield holders will envelop the inmate that is to be extracted and form a protective barrier. Once the shield holders have enveloped the inmate, the nonlethal gunners will cover the sides with the weapons while the apprehension and search members control and restrain the inmate. When the team has the inmate under control, the squad leader will give the order for the team to withdraw. The team withdraws in reverse order (apprehension and search members with the inmate, followed by nonlethal gunners and shield holders). Team members then move backwards, facing the crowd and gripping the shoulder or equipment of the member in front of them.

5-34. Proper equipment that is both offensive and defensive in nature is required for an extraction team. Recommended equipment for an extraction team include—
- Disposable restraints (zip-ties).
- Restraint cutters.
- Pepper spray.
- Helmets with face shields.
- Groin protectors.
- Body Armor.
- Elbow pads.
- Leather gloves.
- Shin protectors.
- Knee pads.
- A video camera.

Forced Cell-Move Team

5-35. The other specialized team is the FCMT. The intent of a forced cell-move is to move an unruly or uncooperative inmate from a cell to another location. This is a difficult task and must not be taken lightly. A forced cell-move must be thoroughly planned, rehearsed, and resourced to ensure the safety of the team members and the inmate.

Chapter 5

5-36. The commander considers a forced cell-move for several reasons. The inmate may refuse to eat, take medication, accept medical attention, get a haircut, keep himself clean, work, or move or rotate cells when ordered to. An inmate may become unruly, a danger to themselves or a cell mate, or may require medical attention but is refusing. An inmate in these situations may also be verbally and physically abusive to facility cadre.

5-37. A typical FCMT is composed of six corrections Soldiers and two support personnel from military police and medical sections specially trained in forced cell-movement. Primarily, the team consists of the following personnel:
- One officer in charge (OIC).
- Five corrections Soldiers.
- One military police investigator.
- One medic.

5-38. Proper equipment that is offensive and defensive in nature is required for an FCMT. Recommended equipment for a FCMT include—
- Helmets with face shields.
- Groin protectors.
- Body Armor.
- Elbow pads.
- Leather gloves.
- Shin guards.
- Knee pads.
- A pinning shield.
- Restraints (hand or leg irons or zip ties).
- A video camera.

Actions Prior to Team Employment

5-39. The OIC gives an operations order to team member five (the team leader) of the FCMT. As a minimum, the operations order should answer the following questions about the incident leading up to the move:
- Did the inmate fail to comply with orders?
- Did the inmate assault cadre or other inmates?
- What is the objective of the forced move?
- Is pepper spray authorized for use?
- Has the inmate been moved before?
- What is the condition of the area where the inmate is currently located?
- Has the inmate tested positive for human immunodeficiency virus (HIV)?
- Does the inmate have a weapon or the materials to make one?
- Is the area barricaded?
- Has he smeared himself with body fluids or other slippery substances?
- Can the inmate be approached without risk to them or others?

5-40. The team is assembled for inspection by the OIC, and the team members are required to brief the OIC on individual duties and responsibilities. A line formation is the customary formation for this inspection. It should take place out of sight of the inmates.

5-41. Each Soldier takes one step forward and briefs the OIC with their rank and name, team member number, their duties and responsibilities, and the equipment they possess. The team member then faces so that the camera can record the number printed on the back of the body armor, and they hold up any special equipment they are to use (see figure 5-1, figure 5-2, and figure 5-3).

Figure 5-1. Recording FCMT member duty position

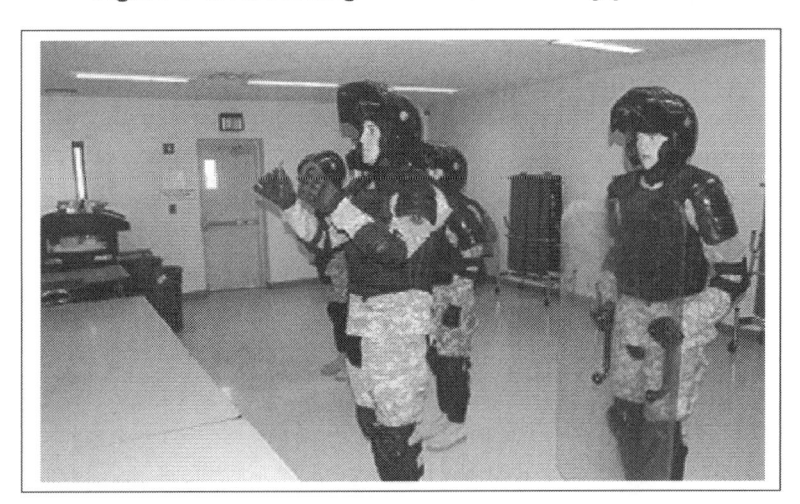

Figure 5-2. Recording FCMT member equipment

Figure 5-3. Recording FCMT member number on armor

Chapter 5

Individual Team Member Responsibilities

5-42. Each FCMT team member of has their own responsibilities during a forced cell-move. The team members must do their designated jobs and work as a team. The following discussion is based on a typical eight member team. As always, situations and needs of the commander may alter what or how missions are executed.

- **Team member one.** During the team inspection, team member one steps forward and briefs the OIC as follows: "I am [rank and name], team member one. My mission is to pin the inmate using the minimum amount of force necessary. I carry the pinning shield." Team member one is the eyes and ears of the team. Their responsibility is to carry the pinning shield up to the cell door and describe the scene with as much detail as possible (especially including anything that may cause harm to the team). The pinning shield is used to protect the team from body fluids thrown at them by the inmate. Team member one describes the scene in the cell to his teammates by turning his head to the right and speaking in a loud voice so that all team members can hear him. A slap on the right shoulder by team member two alerts member one that all team members have heard the information. If member one receives a slap on the left shoulder from team member two, or no slap at all in a timely manner, they repeat the situation report in a loud, clear voice. At a minimum, he must answer the following questions and report them to the team:
  - Does the inmate have a weapon, if so, what kind?
  - Does the inmate appear dry?
  - Is the inmate clothed or wearing extra clothing?
  - Has the inmate smeared anything on his body?
  - Can the inmate's hands be seen?
  - Is the cell barricaded or visibly booby-trapped?
  - Is the cell dry?
  - Are cell furnishings intact?

  The decision to enter the inmate's area with or without the pinning shield is team member one's decision, unless the inmate is known to have a weapon. Should member one decide to enter without the pinning shield, they then enter with both hands held approximately chest high. When team member one is unable to determine if the inmate has a weapon, the pinning shield is used. Charging through the open cell door, team member one drives the inmate to the bunk or ground with the shield. Once pinned and other team members have secured the inmate's arms and legs, team member one secures the inmate's head and ensures that it is not twisted or turned in relation to its natural form. Various pressure points on the inmate's head may be utilized to help subdue them.

- **Team member two.** During the team inspection, team member two steps forward and briefs the OIC as follows: "I am [rank and name], team member two. My mission is to secure the inmate's right arm using the minimum amount of force necessary. I carry one set of hand irons." They then hold the hand irons up for video camera taping and say, "I also carry one canister of pepper spray to be used at the direction of the team OIC." They then hold up the canister for video camera taping and then turn around so that the camera can record the number on the back of the body armor. Team member two lines up directly behind team member one. Member two keeps contact with team member one until they can secure the inmate's strong arm. Once inside the cell, team member two secures the prisoner's strong hand with wrist restraints and announces, "Hands secured" to team member five. If the inmate's strong arm cannot be immediately secured, team member two secures a portion of the inmate's body and progresses to the inmate's strong arm. Once the inmate's hands are secure, they announce, "Hands secured" to team member five.

- **Team member three.** During the team inspection, team member three steps forward and briefs the OIC as follows: "I am [rank and name], team member three. My mission is to secure the inmate's left arm using the minimum amount of force necessary." Team member three then faces so that the camera can record the number on the back of the body armor. Team member three lines up directly behind team member two. Team member three keeps contact with team member two until they can grasp a portion of the inmate's body. They then concentrate on securing the inmate's support hand and assisting team member two in applying hand restraints. Team member three maintains control of the inmate's hands and looks at team member five for further instructions.

- **Team member four.** During the team inspection, team member four steps forward and briefs the OIC as follows: "I am [rank and name], team member four. My mission is to secure the inmate's right leg using the minimum amount of force necessary. I carry one set of leg irons." They hold the leg irons up for the camera to record and then faces so that the camera can record the number on the back of the body armor. Team member four lines up directly behind team member three. Team member four keeps contact with team member three until they can secure a portion of the inmate's body. Team member four concentrates on securing the right leg of the inmate. It is their responsibility to apply the leg irons. Once the legs are secure, member four announces, "Legs secure" to team member five.
- **Team member five (team leader).** Team member five steps forward and briefs the OIC as follows: "I am [rank and name], team member five. My mission is to secure the inmate's left leg using the minimum amount of force necessary. I carry a restraint key (hold up for the camera to view). I am also the team leader for this mission and it is my responsibility to ensure that the team uses the minimum amount of force necessary to subdue the inmate." The team leader then faces so that the camera can record the number on the back of the body armor. Team member five taps team member four on the right shoulder when they have heard the situation report from team member one. If they do not hear the report or need to hear it again, they tap team member four on the left shoulder. Team member five keeps in contact with team member four until they can secure a portion of the inmate's body. Team member five secures the left leg and assists team member four in applying the leg irons. Once they have heard that the hands and legs are secure, team member five signals for the team to conduct a search of the inmate for weapons and contraband. The team leader then directs the team to conduct an equipment check, which is done in place.

Note. At no time is the inmate to be released by any team member during equipment check.

- **Medic.** During the team inspection, the medic briefs the OIC in the following manner: "I am [rank and name], the medic. My mission is to treat all injuries that may occur during the move." The medic follows the instructions given by the OIC. Their mission is to observe the inmate for signs of injury before the forced cell-move and assess the inmate's condition during and after the move.
- **Military police investigator.** The military police investigator is responsible for videotaping the entire forced cell-move. This includes the OIC briefing the operations order, each team member briefing their responsibilities to the OIC, and any medical treatment rendered to the inmate.
- **Officer in charge.** The OIC, usually an E-7 or above, is responsible for ensuring that the team uses the minimum amount of force necessary to subdue the inmate. The OIC is also responsible for ensuring that all necessary precautions have been taken to ensure team and inmate safety. The OIC gives the inmate the initial orders to comply and informs the inmate of the consequences of noncompliance. The OIC does this by placing themselves at the front of the inmate's cell. The orders are not given until they can be enforced by the FCMT (see figure 5-4, page 5-12).

5-43. The following is an example of a prepared statement that is read to the inmate by the OIC: "I am (rank and name), OIC of this team. At this time I am ordering you to lie face down on your bunk (or other designated location) with your head to the rear of the cell. Cross your hands behind your back and cross your feet as the team enters the cell and uses the minimum amount of force necessary to place you in restraints and move you to (give location). Failure on your part to comply with these instructions or to resist the team will result in the use of force, to include pepper spray pepper spray, physical self-defense, and physical restraint. Do you understand these instructions? If so, lie down on the bunk."

5-44. After reading the instructions to the inmate, the OIC faces the camera and states if the inmate complied. The OIC then waits 60 seconds and motions for the team to position itself in front of the inmate's cell. The OIC directs the opening of the cell when the team is positioned at the cell entrance and prepared to enter. The OIC positions himself so that he can observe team entry to and departure from the cell. If pepper spray is authorized, the OIC tells the team when to spray the inmate with pepper spray.

Figure 5-4. OIC with FCMT prior to cell entry

Movement of the Inmate

5-45. Once the FCMT has secured and searched the inmate, team member five commands, "Prepare to lift." Team member one positions their hands to control the inmate's head during the move, and turns the inmate's head toward the wall. Team members two and three position themselves on the inmate's right and left sides. They grasp the wrist or forearm of the team member opposite them to form a platform for the inmate to lie on. Team member four positions himself on the inmate's right side even with the inmate's knees. This places member four in position to control the inmate's legs. Team member five's position is on the inmate's left side and enables them to control the inmate's lower legs and feet. When in position, team member five ensures that all team members are in place before commanding, "Ready, lift."

5-46. On the command "Lift," all team members simultaneously stand, bringing the inmate up with them. They should sandwich the inmate between them to facilitate control. Team member five then commands, "Prepare to turn, ready—turn." The inmate is always turned toward the bunk. If a bunk is not available, team member five should specify which direction to turn the inmate. The inmate is then removed from the cell.

Treating Any Injuries

5-47. Once the inmate is on the tier, outside the cell, team member five commands, "Prepare to lower, team—lower." The team simultaneously lowers the inmate to the floor with the team keeping positive control of the inmate. The medic asks the inmate, "Do you have any injuries at this time?" If the inmate has no injuries, the medic looks at the camera and states, "Inmate [inmate name] appears to have sustained no injuries." If the inmate has sustained injuries, the medic treats those injuries and completes a sworn statement. If pepper spray was employed, the medic decontaminates the inmate using water and paper towels. The medic instructs the inmate to tilt their head to the side, and then proceeds to flush their eyes with water for approximately 5 minutes. The medic then dries the inmate's face.

Placement of the Inmate in a Cell

5-48. Team member five orders an equipment check before returning the inmate to a cell. The team leader then commands, "Prepare to lift, team—lift." Team members position themselves exactly where they were when they removed the inmate from the cell. Next, team members simultaneously lift the inmate and return them to the predetermined cell. They move the inmate into the cell head first with their face toward the bunk. Once inside the cell, team member five commands the team to lower the inmate onto the bunk. Team members then remove the inmate's restraints, keeping positive control of the inmate at all times. Team members use a nonverbal signal (or verbal, if needed) to notify team member five when the restraints are removed. He signals another equipment check. Team members then account for all equipment in place and prepare to exit the cell.

Team Exiting the Cell

5-49. The team exits the cell in the same manner as they entered, but in reverse order. Team member four moves into a position where he can control both of the inmate's legs while team member five moves toward the cell door. When team member four is ready to exit the cell, team member three moves to control the inmate's legs, team member two moves to where they can control both of the inmates arms, and team member one maintains control of the inmate's head. Team member four maintains contact with team member three at all times. When team member three is ready to exit the cell, team member two moves into a position where he can control the inmate's lower body and team member one moves into position to control the inmate's upper body. Using a prearranged, nonverbal signal (or verbal, if needed), the team pulls team members one and two from the cell. The FCMT is prepared to reenter the cell if the inmate attempts to attack team members one and two as they exit the cell. The FCMT remains ready to reenter until the cell door is secured.

This page intentionally left blank.

Appendix A
Metric Conversion Chart

Table A-1 is a metric conversion chart. A complete listing of preferred metric units for general use is contained in Fed-Std-376B.

Table A-1. Metric conversion chart

U.S. Units	Multiplied By	Equals Metric Units
Feet	0.30480	Meters
Inches	2.54000	Centimeters
Inches	0.02540	Meters
Inches	25.40010	Millimeters
Miles (statute)	1.60934	Kilometers
Miles per hour	0.04470	Meter per second
Pounds	0.45359	Kilograms
Yards	0.91440	Meters
Metric Units	**Multiplied By**	**Equals U.S. Units**
Centimeters	0.39370	Inches
Kilometer	0.62137	Miles
Meters per second	2.23700	Miles per hour
Meters	3.28080	Feet
Meters	39.37000	Inches
Meters	1.09361	Yards
Millimeters	0.03937	Inches
Kilograms	2.20460	Pounds

This page intentionally left blank.

Appendix B
Practical Application

It is always best to derive lessons learned from practical operations in the field. These are operations where a measure of success was acquired, along with important lessons learned. The following reflects an actual task force application of the doctrine highlighted in the contents of this manual.

GENERAL INFORMATION

B-1. The purpose of this appendix is to provide task force units and elements with the latest guidance on providing crowd control and preventing civil disturbances.

Note. See figure 4-1 for a symbol key for the figures in the appendix.

B-2. Local civilians often gather in towns or along strategic locations throughout an area of operation to demonstrate grievances or other causes (for example, protesting the apprehension of a fellow citizen, policies of U.S. forces, and policies of government services). Although civilians have the right to assemble, crowd gatherings are predominantly ethnically based, motivated, and influenced. Local civilians can apply for a permit to legally conduct a rally 72 hours in advance as long as their assembly is peaceful and unobtrusive to government services, freedom of movement, or the rights of others. On occasion, information collection can indicate a possibility for violence. In these instances or during spontaneous crowd formations, the task force must provide forces in support of a safe and secure environment or to assist civilian police in preventing unlawful acts. If unlawful acts are committed, detain violators for adjudication under the legal system.

B-3. During lawful assemblies, the task force must make every effort to treat individuals with respect. This means that the task force must engage in peaceful gatherings using interpersonal communication skills. This ensures that demonstrators understand that task force personnel respect their right to lawfully assemble during peaceful demonstrations. When possible, task force engagement of a peaceful assembly should be unobtrusive.

B-4. Take precautions to avoid becoming a catalyst to the civil disturbance. Do not display civil disturbance equipment or weapons, overtly prepare defenses against a crowd, or aggressively violate crowd space, unless presented with information, intelligence, or negative indicators of pending violence.

NEGATIVE INDICATORS OF A POTENTIAL CIVIL DISTURBANCE

B-5. Predictive intelligence is the best indicator of a potential civil disturbance and may provide insight on internal planning, external influences, environmental conditions, or catalyst events that should influence task force planning and response. Any response to negative indicators should be sequential, measured, and focused on deescalating rather than escalating the crowd.

B-6. When people begin to assemble, leaders should pay particular attention to crowd dynamics. If the crowd demeanor or dynamics change from peaceful assembly to unruly behavior or unlawful acts, negative indicators should provide an advance warning and prompt a measured response. Negative indicators of a potential change in crowd dynamics and unlawful activities should prompt immediate countermeasures.

ORIENTATION

B-7. Crowd orientation is very important. Knowing where people are and what they are doing is essential to crowd management. Crowd dynamics change from people milling around and talking among themselves

Appendix B

in isolated groups to a more collective focus concentrated on a single objective (task force personnel, specific agitators or magnets, a government figure, other activity).

MASSING

B-8. The crowd begins to mass or tighten into a large contiguous body from a loose formation to a static congregation located in a more concentrated area. According to the Contagion Theory, if unchecked, massing can provide anonymity and a collective feeling of invulnerability. This change in group dynamics could provide ideal conditions for a civil disturbance (see figure B-1).

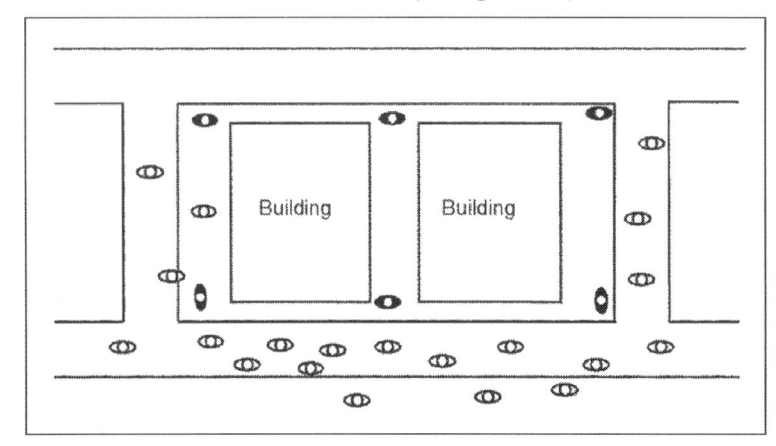

Figure B-1. Crowd massing

CHANTING

B-9. People may begin chanting slogans or yelling ethnically charged rhetoric or obscenities. Because chanting can indicate an increase in crowd intensity, interpreters should be positioned in strategic locations to interpret crowd rhetoric.

SIGNALING

B-10. Signaling occurs when members of the crowd position themselves to communicate and synchronize crowd actions tied to a plan with specific objectives. Signaling may indicate the intent to escalate the message through the use of violent or unlawful acts.

BLOCKING

B-11. The crowd may attempt to block public thoroughfares (for example, entrances and exits to public buildings, main supply routes, community streets, or other traffic areas that may degrade freedom of movement or similar actions). This escalates the level of attention that is given to the crowd's message or prevents the freedom of movement to opposing persons or groups.

ARMING

B-12. Any signs that the crowd is arming itself with objects (bottles, rocks, sticks) are a clear indication of impending danger to the task force and other civilians. Sometimes members of the crowd can be seen handing out bottles or other weapons to others in the crowd. Arming demonstrates intent toward violence and is unlawful.

OUTSIDE INFLUENCE

B-13. The presence of people from outside the community may indicate more sophisticated planning and resources than would otherwise be expected from local community members. Outside people may feel insulated from responsibility for local actions and, therefore, provide a dangerous catalyst for a violent civil disturbance.

AGITATORS AND INSTIGATORS

B-14. Agitators and instigators are common elements associated with civil disturbances. They often provide a catalyst to incite the crowd toward violence. Whether spewing rhetoric or committing unlawful acts, their continued presence will fuel potential strife.

ABSENCE OF CHILDREN

B-15. Recent civil disturbances have shown that even when children were initially present at a rally, they were absent before the civil disturbance erupted with violence. While the presence of children is not a guarantee of a peaceful assembly, the removal of children from a rally may provide early warning for a pending escalation of hostilities or a full-blown riot.

PREVENTION OF CROWD ESCALATION

B-16. If task force personnel believe, based on intelligence or negative indicators, that a crowd is planning to, or may spontaneously, riot they should immediately engage crowd participants using the preventive tactics, techniques, and procedures.

B-17. The force executing these preventive techniques can include a number of civil disturbance teams and elements capable of executing the tasks shown in figure B-2; figure B-3, page B-4; and figure B-4, page B-4. These figures demonstrate a full range of crowd control teams and elements, to include camera teams with interpreters, checkpoints, quick reaction force, riot control formation, NLW teams, apprehension teams, blocking teams, and detainee evacuation, as required. Figure B-2, figure B-3, and figure B-4 illustrate the evolution of a crowd formation and the recommended positioning of teams and elements to engage people as they congregate. Included with each security team is a designated camera or video recorder.

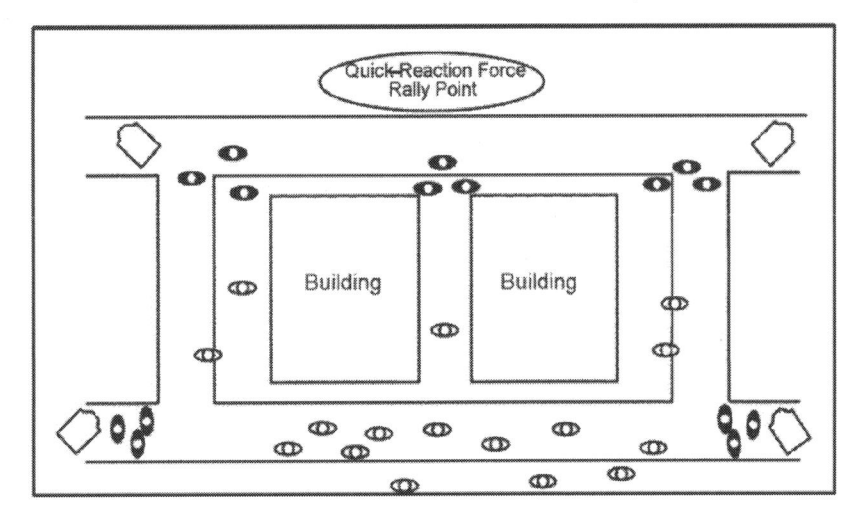

Figure B-2. Early contact and unobtrusive crowd control measures

B-18. Depending on the situation and crowd dynamics, it may not be necessary to establish all crowd control teams and elements, but they should be included in planning. Regardless of task organization, teams and elements must be prepared to execute the crowd control and civil disturbance tasks. The order to execute the following tactics, techniques, and procedures should be tailored based on local conditions.

Appendix B

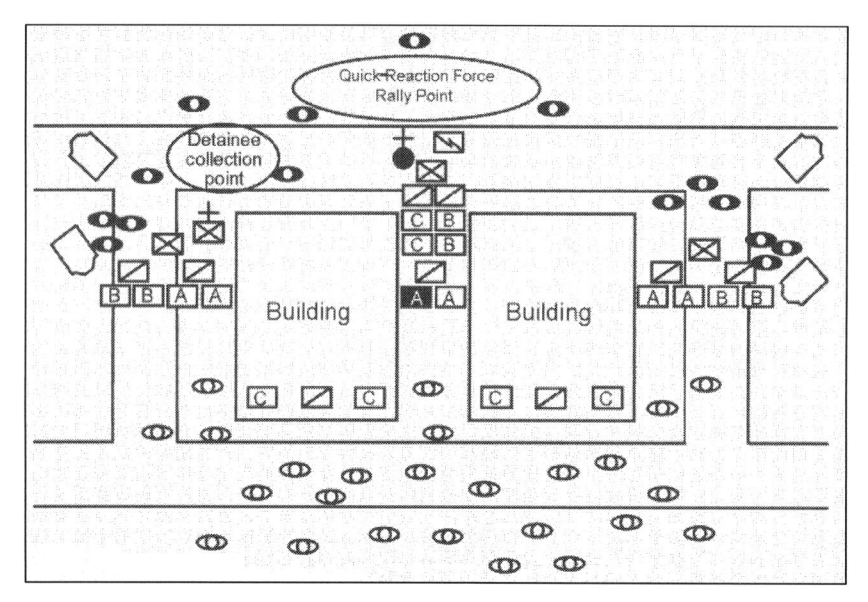

Figure B-3. More obtrusive engagement as the crowd demonstrates negative indicators

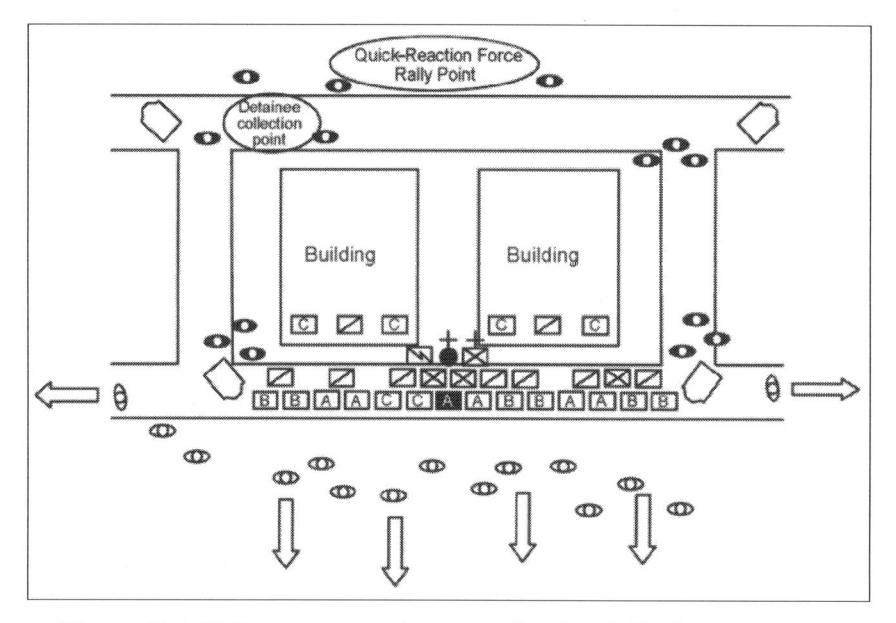

Figure B-4. Full engagement as crowd unlawfully demonstrates

EARLY CONTACT

B-19. Engaging people as a crowd forms is essential to prevention. Whether based on intelligence or negative indicators, people should be engaged early, before the crowd masses as shown in figure B-1, page B-2, rather than waiting until after the crowd masses as shown in figure B-2, page B-3. Early contact will assist task forces in personalizing their interaction and ensuring that people understand their presence is known, documented, and can be linked to their actions.

B-20. Cameras are one of the best tools for preventing civil disturbances. The use of cameras to document crowd formations, particularly lens-size groups (small enough to fit in a single photo), will personalize contact and eliminate feelings of anonymity among the crowd. People whose identity has been documented will think twice before committing unlawful acts. Even without documenting names, photo analysis can identify people associated with the civil disturbance, especially those who participated as crowd instigators, agitators, or those who may have committed unlawful acts.

B-21. As people begin to gather in and along streets, camera teams should be deployed as unobtrusively as possible to engage people before they congregate in mass. As depicted in figure B-2, page B-3, camera teams should consist of two Soldiers with an interpreter and be employed in a widely dispersed pattern. Such small, dispersed camera teams are less likely to intrude on lawful rallies or create invasive friction that might become a catalyst to a civil disturbance.

B-22. As the crowd begins to demonstrate negative indicators for a possible civil disturbance (see figure B-3 camera teams should become more invasive by actively engaging groups to take their pictures. Camera teams should focus cameras on instigators, agitators, or magnets (personnel that garner respect or compliance from the crowd). If a person is purposely avoiding the camera, even if their activities are lawful, the team should take special measures to obtain their picture. Each time a camera team takes a picture of a person or group of people, they must immediately engage them using the warning outlined in paragraph B-25.

B-23. Once the crowd has massed and displays negative indicators or begins to riot, camera teams should immediately move behind the riot formation line (see figure B-3). It is essential; however, that camera teams continue to document the event, focusing on people who are committing illegal acts such as arming themselves, throwing objects, and assaulting task force personnel.

B-24. Immediately following a crowd control or civil disturbance mission, photos must be consolidated, processed, and submitted to the task force analysis and control element for analysis. A near real-time analysis will provide immediate intelligence for ongoing operations to prevent subsequent civil disturbances or to detain violators from the previous operation.

CROWD WARNING

B-25. Once the team has taken a picture of a person or group of people, they should warn the crowd that as individuals they would be held accountable for their actions. Using an interpreter, the camera team leader will make solid eye contact with the person or group and state the following warning: "We have your picture. You will be held accountable for your actions. If you commit an unlawful act, you will be detained, if not today, tomorrow. Blocking roads or access to public buildings is unlawful."

LIMIT CROWD SIZE

B-26. Persons seeking to conduct a rally must apply for a permit through civilian authorities at least 72 hours prior to the meeting. If a rally has not been lawfully scheduled through civilian authorities, or if it has, but is demonstrating negative indicators and is turning into a civil disturbance, task force units and elements should attempt to limit the crowd or separate gatherings under 10 people (see figure B-2, page B-3). Walking patrols can assist camera teams in breaking up large groups. Walking patrols should operate in conjunction with camera teams. This will ensure that camera teams can accurately document and provide the aforementioned warning to prevent further escalation of crowd size or behavior.

CLEAR ROUTES

B-27. Routes should be considered key terrain and must be controlled by the task force to retain the initiative. Note how a quick-reaction force divides to clear side streets between protected buildings in figure B-3, page B-4. Blocking routes or public thoroughfares is not only illegal, but severely restrictive to civil disturbance operations. Routes must remain open to allow movement of task force and elements, whether it is for camera teams during early contact or for the quick-reaction force to respond during an actual civil disturbance. Because blocking routes is illegal, camera teams must document responsible persons for immediate or subsequent detention and legal processing.

ISOLATE THE AREA

B-28. As depicted in figure B-2, page B-3 checkpoints should be established to isolate the area. While checkpoints can prevent people from entering the isolated area, they should never prevent people from

Appendix B

exiting the area. When trapped, people may escalate the level of violence out of fear, anger, or desperation. When placing checkpoints, leaders should find a location that is close enough to limit the number of persons being isolated, but far enough away that they will not draw a crowd from people within the isolated area. Checkpoints are essential to preventing others from joining the already gathered crowds. These checkpoints must provide adequate space for processing vehicles in both directions; but when limited by space or other considerations, it should simply block traffic trying to enter the isolated area. Improve force protection measures in and around checkpoints as necessary. Strategically placed checkpoints can provide numerous countermeasures to prevent and control a civil disturbance or to identify and detain persons who may have committed unlawful acts during the riot. Use checkpoints to prevent potential participants from joining the crowd or civil disturbance. Checkpoints should also prevent any activity that may commingle ethnic groups. The checkpoint must process people who departing the area by documenting personal and vehicle information with the pictures of all occupants in front of or adjacent to the vehicle.

ESTABLISH LETHAL OVERWATCH

B-29. The mentality of taking the high ground is just as important in civil disturbance operations as in any other type of operation. Although quick-reaction force assets on the ground have nonlethal and lethal capabilities, it is critical to ensure their safety by deploying marksman/observer teams, as shown with the C-team depicted on top of the buildings in figure B-3, page B-4 and figure B-4, page B-4.

DETAIN PERSONS COMMITTING UNLAWFUL ACTS

B-30. The detention and legal processing of persons who commit unlawful acts, against task force or local laws sends a clear message that all people will be held accountable for their actions. Immediately detain persons who are committing unlawful acts and are isolated or easily accessible, unless this would create a catalyst event or endanger the apprehension team. If it is not feasible to immediately detain them, a picture with relevant information should be forwarded for analysis and inclusion on the detain list for their detention at a later date and time. Remember, as stated in the warning, they will be detained, if not today, tomorrow. Detainees should be quickly relocated to the forward processing site for detainee evacuation (see figure B-4, page B-4). Detainee evacuation sites should be behind the control formations to prevent any interference from the local population. Sites should be positioned at two separate locations, such as at the end of a town or located along a main supply route. All people who are detained based on solid evidence of a crime (for example, pictures of them armed with dangerous objects, blocking a road, assaulting task force members) will be turned over to local authorities for legal processing. When executing a mission based on the detain list, do not show unauthorized persons the list or separate pictures from the list.

QUICK-REACTION FORCE

B-31. The quick-reaction force should be positioned with easy access to decisive points to interdict formations or gathering of crowds, support checkpoints, or provide sustained operations in support of early contact teams. Notice in figure B-2, page B-3, how the QRF is positioned out of direct sight of the crowd until employment becomes necessary. Quick-reaction force personnel are readily organized, equipped, and easily moved into position to move between buildings and through obstacles (see figure B-3, page B-4).

B-32. At this point, if the crowd ignores verbal orders, nonlethal munitions from appropriate standoff distances could be used to influence and motivate the crowd to comply. Use of nonlethal munitions could prevent the necessity for quick-reaction force personnel to come into direct physical contact with the crowd. Early positioning of the quick-reaction force could become a catalyst event that may instigate a civil disturbance.

B-33. Assembling directly in front of the protected buildings demonstrates to the crowd that there is strength in numbers and the quick-reaction force is determined to disperse the crowd from the area. As a reminder, remove the flanking checkpoints that may block the dispersal of the crowd.

Glossary

The glossary lists acronyms with Army or joint definitions.

SECTION I – ACRONYMS AND ABBREVIATIONS

AA	assembly area
ADP	Army doctrine publication
ADRP	Army doctrine reference publication
AR	Army regulation
ATP	Army techniques publication
ATTN	attention
CFR	Code of Federal Regulation
COA	course of action
CONUS	continental United States
DA	Department of the Army
DC	District of Columbia
DCSA	Defense Support of Civil Authorities
DD	Departement of Defense
DM	designated marksman
DOD	Department of Defense
DODD	Department of Defense directive
DODI	Department of Defense instruction
FCMT	forced cell move team
Fed	federal
FM	field manual
G-2	Assistant Chief of Staff, Intelligence
GRM	graduated-response matrix
HIV	human immunodeficiency virus
HN	host nation
IPB	intelligence preparation of the battlefield
JP	joint publication
LEA	law enforcement agency
METT-TC	mission, enemy, terrain and weather, troops and support available, time available, and civil considerations
MI	military intelligence
MISO	military information support operations
MO	Missouri
MSCoE	Maneuver Support Center of Excellence
MWD	military working dog
MTTP	multi-Service tactics, techniques, and procedures
NGR	National Guard regulation
No.	number
NLW	nonlethal weapons
OCONUS	outside the continental United States
OIC	officer in charge
PIO	police intelligence operations
PSG	platoon sergeant

RCA	riot control agent
ROE	rules of engagement
RUF	rules for the use of force
S-2	intelligence officer
SJA	staff judge advocate
SOP	standard operating procedures
Std	standard
U.S.	United States
USAMPS	United States Army Military Police School
USC	United States Code

SECTION II – TERMS

None

References

REQUIRED PUBLICATIONS

These are the sources quoted or paraphrased in this publication.

ADRP 1-02. *Terms and Military Symbols.* 24 September 2013.

JP 1-02. *Department of Defense Dictionary of Military and Associated Terms.* 8 November 2010.

RELATED PUBLICATIONS

These documents contain relevant supplemental information.

ARMY PUBLICATIONS

Most Army doctrinal publications are available online at <www.apd.army.mil>.

ADP 3-28. *Defense Support of Civil Authorities.* 26 July 2012.

ADRP 3-28. *Defense Support of Civil Authorities.* 14 June 2013.

ADRP 5-0. *The Operations Process.* 17 May 2012.

AR 190-14. *Carrying Firearms and Use of Force for Law Enforcement and Security Duties.* 12 March 1993.

AR 380-13. *Acquisition and Storage of Information Concerning Nonaffiliated Persons and Organizations.* 30 September 1974.

AR 381-10. *US Army Intelligence Activities.* 3 May 2007.

ATTP 3-39.34. *Military Working Dogs.* 10 May 2011.

FM 2-01.3. *Intelligence Preparation of the Battlefield/Battlespace.* 15 October 2009.

FM 3-06. *Urban Operations.* 26 October 2006.

FM 3-22.40. *Multiservice Tactics, Techniques, and Procedures (MTTP) for Tactical Employment of Nonlethal Weapons (NLW).* 24 October 2007.

FM 3-39. *Military Police Operations.* 26 August 2013.

FM 5-19. *Composite Risk Management.* 21 August 2006.

FM 27-10. *The Law of Land Warfare.* 18 July 1956.

TC 3-19.5. *Nonlethal Weapons Training.* 5 November 2009.

JOINT PUBLICATIONS

Most joint publications are available online at <www.dtic.mil/doctrine/new_pubs/jointpub.htm>.

JP 1-04. *Legal Support to Military Operations.* 17 August 2011.

JP 3-28. *Defense Support to Civil Support.* 31 July 2013.

OTHER PUBLICATIONS

32 CFR, Part 215. *Employment of Military Resources in the Event of Civil Disturbances.*

Constitution of the United States.

DODD 3025.18. *Defense Support of Civil Authorities (DCSA).* 29 December 2010.

DODD 5200.27. *Acquisition of Information Concerning Persons and Organizations not Affiliated with the Department of Defense.* 7 January 1980.

DODI 3025.21. *Defense Support of Civilian Law Enforcement.* 27 February 2013.

Executive Order 12333. *United States Intelligence Activities.* 4 December 1981.

Fed-Std 376B. *Preferred Metric Units for General Use for the Federal Government.* 27 January 1993.

House Joint Resolution 1292. 6 June 1968.

References

NGR 500-1. *National Guard Domestic Operations.* 13 June 2008.
10 USC, Subtitle A, Part I, Chapter 15, Section 331. *Federal Aid for State Governments.*
10 USC, Subtitle A, Part I, Chapter 15, Section 332. *Use of Militia and Armed Forces to Enforce Federal Authority.*
10 USC, Subtitle A, Part I, Chapter 15, Section 333. *Interference With State and Federal Law.*
10 USC, Subtitle A, Part I, Chapter 15, Section 334. *Proclamation to Disperse.*
18 USC, Part I, Chapter 67, Section 1385. *Use of Army and Air Force as a Posse Comitatus.*

PRESCRIBED FORMS

None.

REFERENCED FORMS

DEPARTMENT OF THE ARMY FORMS

DA Forms are available on the APD web site: <www.apd.army.mil>.
DA Form 2028. *Recommended Changes to Publications and Blank Forms.*
DA Form 4137. *Evidence/Property Custody Document.*

DEPARTMENT OF DEFENSE FORMS

DD Forms are available from the OSD web site: <http://www.dtic.mil/whs/directives/infomgt/forms/index.htm>.
DD Form 2708. *Receipt for Pre-Trial/Post Trial Prisoner or Detained Person.*

WEB SITES

Army Knowledge Online, Doctrine and Training Publications Web site, <https://armypubs.us.army.mil/doctrine/index.html>, accessed on 28 January 2014.
Army Publishing Directorate, Army Publishing Updates Web site, <http://www.apd.army.mil/AdminPubs/new_subscribe.asp>, accessed on 28 January 2014.
Army Publishing Directorate Web Site, <www.apd.army.mil>, accessed on 28 January 2014.
Joint Electronic Library Web site, <www.dtic.mil/doctrine/new_pubs/jointpub.htm>, accessed on 28 January 2014.

RECOMMENDED READINGS

These sources contain relevant supplemental information.

ARMY PUBLICATIONS

Most Army doctrinal publications are available online at <www.apd.army.mil>.
ADP 3-0. Unified Land Operations. 10 October 2011.
ADRP 3-0. Unified Land Operations. 16 May 2012.
FM 3-13. Inform and Influence Activities. 25 January 2013.
FM 3-53. Military Information Support Operations. 4 January 2013.

OTHER PUBLICATIONS

Uniform Code of Military Justice.
10 USC, Chapter 18. *Military Support for Civilian Law Enforcement Agencies.*

Index

Entries are by page number.

A

accountability, 5-3
agendas, 1-3, 1-8
air patrols, 2-19
analysis, 1-7, 2-4, 2-8, 2-10, 2-11, 5-3, B-4, B-5, B-6
anarchists, 1-2, 1-6
anonymous, 1-3
antiglobalization, 1-2
apprehension team, 2-8, 2-20, 2-21, 2-22, 4-8, 5-6, B-3
arming, B-2, B-5

B

ballistic riot face shield, 3-16
barricades, 1-7, 1-8, 2-16, 5-1
baton baton blocking techniques, 3-7
   high block, 3-7
   low block, 3-7
   middle block, 3-9
   strong-side block, 3-8
   support-side block, 3-9
baton carries, 3-5
   two-hand carry, 3-5
behavior, 1-4, 1-5, 1-6, 1-7, 2-5, 2-7, 2-13, 2-21, 3-10, 3-11, 3-12, 3-13, 3-14, 3-15, 5-2, B-1, B-5
blocking, 2-16, 2-20, 2-21, 3-5, 3-7, 3-8, 3-9, B-2, B-3, B-5, B-6
by-the-number commands, 2-19

C

cadre behavior, 5-2
cameras, 2-8, 2-16, B-4, B-5
casual crowds, 1-6
catalyst, B-1, B-3, B-5, B-6
chanting, 1-4, 1-7, B-2
checkpoints, B-3, B-5, B-6
chemical irritants, 1-5, 5-3, 5-4
children, 1-9, B-3
civil law enforcement, 2-21
civil unrest, 1-1
clear routes, B-5
COA
   See course of action (COA), 2-4

commands, 2-8, 2-19, 3-2, 3-18, 4-3, 4-5, 4-6, 4-7, 4-9, 4-10, 4-11, 4-12, 4-13, 4-15, 4-17, 4-21, 4-22, 4-27, 4-28, 4-30, 4-33, 4-38, 5-12
company echelons and wedge formations, 4-30
company line formation, 4-30
company line formations with support, 4-29
company line in depth formation, 4-28
company line in mass formation, 4-28
containment, 1-5, 2-18
control force, 1-1, 1-4, 1-5, 1-6, 1-7, 1-8, 1-9, 2-1, 2-4, 2-5, 2-7, 2-13, 2-16, 2-17, 2-19, 2-20, 2-21, 2-22, 3-1, 3-2, 3-7, 3-15, 3-16, 3-18, 4-1, 4-2, 4-3, 4-4, 4-5, 4-6, 4-7, 4-8, 4-11, 4-19, 4-28, 4-37, 5-1, 5-2, 5-3, 5-6, 5-7
control force team, 5-3
correctional facility cadre, 5-6
course of action (COA), 2-1, 2-11, 5-3
crowd assessment, 2-4
crowd control, 1-5, 2-1, 2-6, 2-7, 2-12, 2-15, 2-16, 2-18, 3-1, 3-17, 3-18, 4-1, 4-2, 4-3, 4-4, 4-9, 4-12, 4-19, 4-21, 4-30, B-1, B-3, B-5
crowd control options, 2-15
crowd dispersal, 1-3, 4-2, 5-5
crowd types, 1-6
   agitated, 1-6
   casual, 1-6
   mob-like or riotous, 1-6
   sighting, 1-6
crowds, 1-2, 1-3, 1-4, 1-5, 1-6, 1-7, 1-8, 2-4, 2-5, 2-6, 2-12, 2-16, 2-19, 4-1, 4-3, B-6

D

deliberate operation, 2-15
demonstrations, 1-1, 1-6, 1-7, 2-5, 2-16, 4-7, 4-8, B-1
Department of Defense (DOD), 2-4
deployment, 2-7
designated marksmen (DM), 2-7

designated marksmen teams, 4-2, 4-8
detain list, B-6
dispersal process, 1-3
   coercion dispersal, 1-3
   emergency dispersal, 1-3
   routine dispersal, 1-3
dispersing, 2-5, 2-17, 4-2
dissemination of chemical irritants, 5-4
   aerosol method, 5-4
   blasting method, 5-4
   fogging method, 5-5
   multipurpose grenade method, 5-5
   projectile method, 5-5
   pyrotechnic method, 5-4
DM
   See designated marksmen (DM), 2-7
DM teams
   See designated marksmen teams, 4-2

E

expandable riot baton, 3-5, 3-6, 3-11, 3-12, 3-18
explosives, 1-8
extraction teams, 2-7, 2-22, 4-3, 4-7, 5-7

F

FCMT
   See forced cell-move team (FCMT), 5-7
fight-or-flight, 1-4, 2-17, 2-18
final phase, 1-3
fire, 1-3, 1-6, 1-7, 1-8, 1-9, 2-11, 2-19, 3-18, 4-1, 4-2, 4-8, 5-4
firearms, 1-8, 2-12, 2-15, 3-18
FMCT
   See forced cell move team (FCMT), 5-10
   See forced cell-move team (FCMT), 5-8, 5-11, 5-12, 5-13
forced cell move team (FCMT) team member five, 5-12
forced cell-move team (FCMT), 5-1
   inspection, 5-8, 5-10
   medic, 5-11

Index

officer in charge, 5-8, 5-10, 5-11
team member five, 5-11, 5-12, 5-13
team member four, 5-11, 5-12
team member one, 5-10
team member three, 5-10, 5-13
team member two, 5-10, 5-13

G

gathering, 1-1, 1-2, 1-3, 1-4, 1-7, 2-4, 2-5, 2-8, 2-12, 2-15, 2-18, 2-22, 5-2, B-1, B-5, B-6
  assembly process, 1-2
  impromptu, 1-2, 2-5
  organized, 1-1, 1-2, 1-4, 1-7, 1-9, 2-5, 2-20, 4-1
graduated response matrix (GRM), 2-10
graduated-response matrix (GRM), 2-9
grievance protest, 5-2
GRM
  See graduated response matrix (GRM), 2-10

H

hand-and-arm signals, 4-4, 4-5
HN
  See host nation (HN), 2-3, 2-6
hostages, 2-19, 5-2
humanitarian assistance, 2-10

I

interval and distance, 4-7

L

law enforcement agencies, 2-3
law enforcement sources, 2-3
lethal overwatch, 3-1, 4-2, 4-8, B-6
lethal protection, 2-7, 4-8

M

massing, 1-8, B-2
military police investigator, 5-8, 5-11
military sources, 2-4
military transport vehicles, 2-19
military working dog (MWD), 2-7
mob, 1-4, 1-6, 1-7, 1-8, 1-9, 2-13, 4-2, 4-8
Molotov cocktails, 1-8
monitoring, 2-16
motorized patrols, 2-19
multiple riots, 5-2

N

negative indicators, B-1, B-3, B-4, B-5
negotiated management, 1-3, 2-6, 2-7
negotiations, 2-7
NLW
  See nonlethal weapons (NLW), 2-12, 2-13, 3-1, 3-18, 4-1, 4-2, 4-4, B-3
nonballistic riot face shield, 3-16
nonlethal weapons (NLW), 2-7, 2-12, 2-13, 3-1, 3-18, 4-1, 4-2, 4-4, B-3
nonviolent tactics, 1-7, 5-1

O

officer in charge, 5-8, 5-10, 5-11, 5-12
OIC
  See officer in charge, 5-8, 5-10, 5-11, 5-12
open sources, 2-3
orientation, B-1

P

patrol routes, 2-19
pepper spray, 2-13, 5-3, 5-8, 5-10, 5-11, 5-12
photographic record, 2-8
physical barriers, 1-8
planned violent disturbances, 5-1
planning process, 1-4, 2-6, 2-12, 5-2
plans, 2-1, 2-5, 2-19, 4-2, 5-2, 5-3
platoon, 2-20, 4-2, 4-4, 4-11, 4-12, 4-13, 4-15, 4-17, 4-18, 4-19, 4-20, 4-21, 4-22, 4-25, 4-26, 4-27, 4-28, 4-29, 4-30, 4-33, 4-36, 4-38, 5-6
platoon diamond and circle formations, 4-18, 4-27
platoon echelon right and left formations, 4-13, 4-23
platoon formations, 4-11, 4-29
  four squads, 4-19
  three squads, 4-11
platoon line formation, 4-11, 4-12, 4-13, 4-16, 4-19, 4-20, 4-21, 4-22, 4-28, 4-37
platoon wedge formation, 4-15, 4-25
platoon wedge formation with general support, 4-16
platoon wedge with direct support, 4-18, 4-27
platoon wedge with general support, 4-26
platoon wedge with lateral support, 4-17, 4-26
platoon wedge with one support squad, 4-27
political grievances, 1-1
predeployment, 2-11
predictive intelligence, B-1
preparation and training, 5-2
proclamation, 2-17, 4-1
psychological operations (PSYOP), 2-12
PSYOP
  See psychological operations (PSYOP), 2-12

R

rate of march, 4-6
RCA
  See riot control agent (RCA), 2-7, 2-9, 2-11, 2-13, 2-17, 4-11, 5-1, 5-3, 5-6
religious-based fighting factions, 1-1
reserve forces, 3-1, 4-3, 4-8
responsibilities, 1-4, 1-5, 2-6, 5-7, 5-8, 5-10, 5-11
riot baton, 1-5, 2-13, 3-1, 3-3, 3-4, 3-5, 3-7, 3-8, 3-9, 3-10, 3-11, 3-12, 3-13, 3-14, 3-15, 3-18, 5-6
riot baton retention, 3-15, 3-16
riot baton striking techniques, 3-10
  one-hand forward strike, 3-10
  one-hand, reverse strike, 3-11, 3-12
  two-hand, front jab, 3-14
  two-hand, middle strike, 3-15
  two-hand, rear jab, 3-14
  two-hand, strong-side, horizontal strike, 3-12
  two-hand, support-side, horizontal strike, 3-13
riot control agent (RCA), 1-4, 2-7, 2-9, 2-11, 2-13, 2-17, 4-11, 5-1, 5-3, 5-6
riot gear, 5-6
riot shield, 2-13, 3-1, 3-2, 3-3, 3-16, 3-17, 3-18, 4-4, 4-7, 4-8, 5-6
riots, 1-1, 1-2, 1-7, 5-2
rocks, 1-8, 3-16, B-2
ROE

Index

See rules of engagement (ROE), 1-6, 2-6, 2-11, 2-12, 4-2
rules of engagement (ROE), 1-6, 2-6, 2-11, 2-12, 4-2

S

sample proclamation, 2-17
scalable effects process, 2-8
show of force, 2-8, 2-11, 2-12, 2-17, 4-1
sniper, 1-9, 2-7, 2-8, 2-11, 2-19, 4-1, 4-8
SOP
   See standing operating procedure (SOP), 5-3, 5-6, 5-7

squad formations, 4-9
   assembly formation, 4-10
   circle formation, 4-10
   diamond formation, 4-10
   echelon formation, 4-9
   line formation, 4-9
   wedge formation, 4-10
standing operating procedure (SOP), 5-2, 5-3, 5-6, 5-7
standoff distance, 4-1, B-6

T

tap-down technique, 3-18
thrown objects, 1-8, 2-17, 2-19, 3-16, 3-17
tracing-C technique, 3-15

U

unanimous, 1-3
unorganized riots, 5-2

V

vehicles, 1-8, 1-9, 2-8, 2-16, 2-18, 2-19, 2-20, 2-21, 4-4, 4-5, 4-7, 4-33, 4-36
violent tactics, 5-1

W

walking patrols, B-5
war, 1-7, 3-15
war-game, 2-10, 2-12
weapon positions, 4-5
   safe-port arms, 4-5
wooden riot baton, 3-5, 3-18

This page intentionally left blank.

ATP 3-39.33
21 April 2014

By order of the Secretary of the Army:

RAYMOND T. ODIERNO
General, United States Army
Chief of Staff

Official:

GERALD B. O'KEEFE
Administrative Assistant to the
Secretary of the Army
1408007

DISTRIBUTION:

Active Army, Army National Guard, and United States Army Reserve: Distributed in electronic media only (EMO).

★ WE STRIVE ★

...To bring you THE BEST HOW-TO BOOKS ★ IN THE WORLD ★

If you enjoyed this one, please TAKE A MOMENT to LEAVE A REVIEW at:

★ AMZN.COM/1987575466

Thank you!

CARLILE MEDIA - WWW.CARLILE.MEDIA - A DIVISION OF CREADYNE DEVELOPMENTS LLC

FOR MORE TOP-FLIGHT MILITARY BOOKS

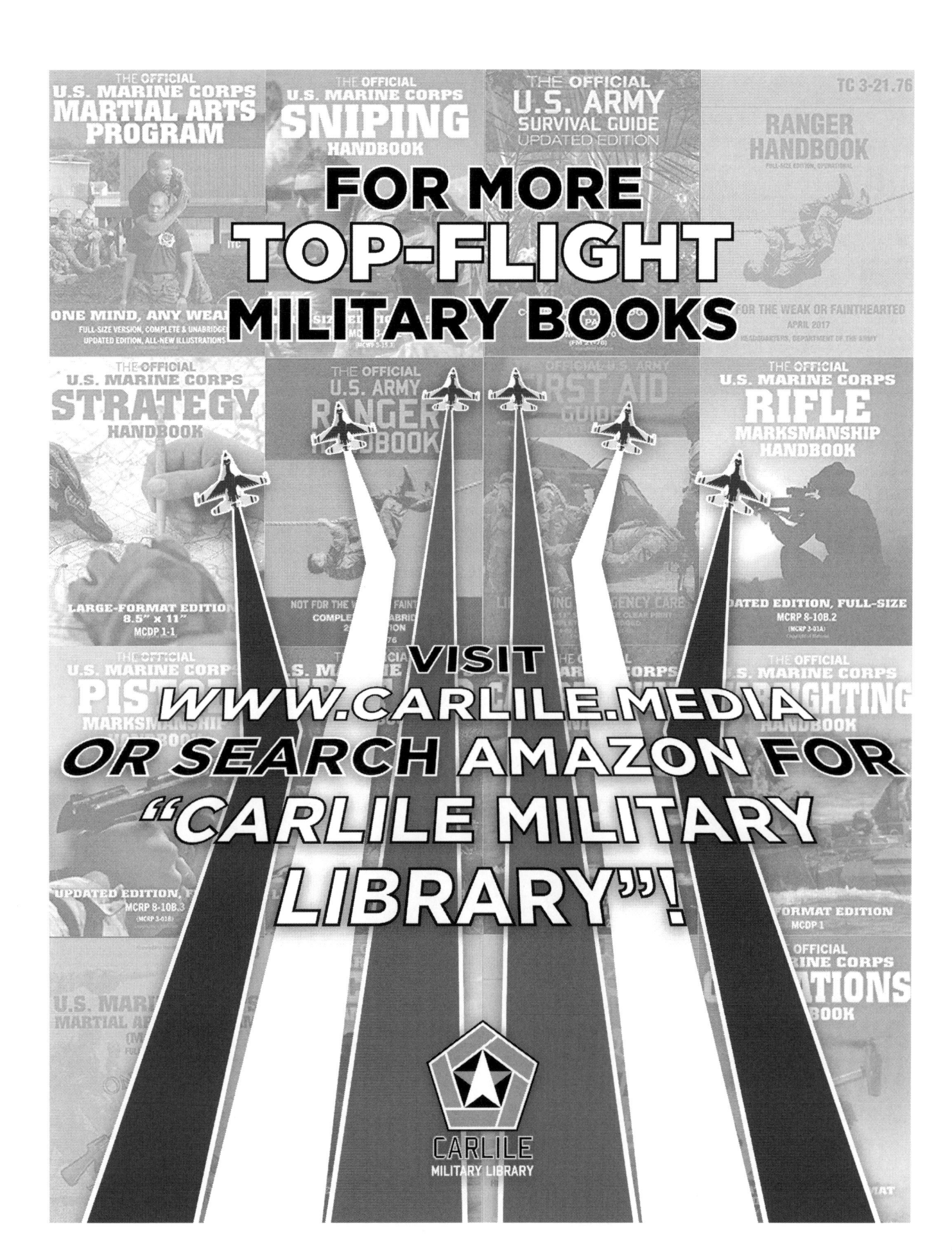

VISIT WWW.CARLILE.MEDIA OR SEARCH AMAZON FOR "CARLILE MILITARY LIBRARY"!

CARLILE
MILITARY LIBRARY